American Wilderness
THE NATIONAL PARKS

Edited by

Letitia Burns O'Connor
& Dana Levy

Introduction by

Michael Duchemin

Essays by

Susan Burke, Leslie Croyder, Mike Macy, Susan J. Tweit

Principal Photography by

Tom Bean

Craig Blacklock

Liz Hymans

David Muench

Marc Muench

Pat O'Hara

Mike Sedam

Scott Smith

UNIVERSE

Tom Bean: 28, 33 left, 37, 52 bottom, 57 right, 63, 84 left, 86 left, 87 right, 90 right, 92 right, 97, 103 top left, 106 left, 115 right

Zandria Muench Beraldo: 17 right

Craig Blacklock: 7, second from top, 24 left and center, 29, 30, 31, 32, 33 right, 34, 36 top right and bottom, 64 right, 70, 89, 114 bottom left and right, 120 right

Fred Hirschmann: 94, 95

Liz Hymans: 7 top, third from top, 14–15, 18 left, 20 top, 38 bottom, 44–45, 46 bottom, 48–50, 52 top, 54 bottom right, 56–57 bottom, 68 bottom, 74, 78 right, 98–99, 104–105 bottom, 108–109, 119 right, 132 left

David Muench: 1, 6, 16 right, 17 left, 18 right, 24 right, 25, 26, 27, 36 top left, 39, 40, 41, 42, 43, 45 right, 46 top, 47, 55, 56 top, 58, 60 left, 64 left, 65, 69, 75 right, 76 left, 81, 102, 103 right, 110, 115 left, 117 right, 121, 129, 130–131, 134

Marc Muench: 85 left, 86 right, 88, 103 bottom left, 113. 119 left

Pat O'Hara: 7 fifth from top, 15 right, 16, 20 left and center, 21, 53 left, 54 top right, 78 left, 79 bottom right, 82 top, 83 right, 84 right, 85 right, 87 left, 90 left, 91, 92 right, 93, 96, 100, 101, 111, 112, 116, 117 left, 120 left, 125, 126, 127, 128 right

Doug Perrin: 22 top, bottom left

Mike Sedam: 7 fourth from top, bottom, 45 right, 53 right, 59 top, 62 bottom, 72–73, 76–77, 79 right, 80–81, 82–83 bottom, 114 top, 118, 122–123, 128 left, 130 left, 132 right, 133

Scott Smith: 2–3, 19, 20 lower right, 38 top, 51, 54 left, 57 top left, 59 bottom, 60–61, 61, 62 top, 66, 67, 68 top, 74–75, 79 top left, 105 top, 106 right, 107

Masa Ushioda: 22 right, 23

Published by
Universe Publishing,
A Division of Rizzoli International Publications, Inc.
300 Park Avenue South
New York, NY 10010
www.rizzoliusa.com

American Wilderness: The National Parks was produced by Perpetua Press, Los Angeles.
Edited by Letitia B. O'Connor
Designed by Dana Levy

2009 2010 2011 2012 / 10 9 8 7 6 5 4 3 2 1

Printed in China

ISBN-13: 978-0-7893-9968-7

Library of Congress Catalog Control Number: 2008933173

Front Cover: Mike Sedam, North Cascades National Park
Back Cover: Marc Muench, Yosemite National Park
PAGE 1: Rain curtain over the Grand Canyon backlit by the setting sun

FOLDOUT: Sunrise at Mesa Arch, Canyonlands National Park

Fallen whitebark pine, Grand Teton National Park

Touring the National Parks: An American Tradition

by Michael Duchemin

MAGINE YOURSELF TAKING IN THE STUNNING SCENERY AND MAGNIFICENT NATURAL FEATURES OF CALIFORNIA'S YOSEMITE NATIONAL PARK. MARVEL AT THE panoramic view of the glacier-carved canyon from Inspiration Point. Applaud the thunder of springtime ice and melting snow cascading over Yosemite Falls. Feel mesmerized by the mist rising off the Merced River. Drink in the scent of morning meadow dew. Retire from the hot sun to walk among the shadows of Giant Sequoias in Mariposa Grove. Travel through these pages and discover the fascinating natural wonders of *American Wilderness: The National Parks.*

From the summit of Cadillac Mountain on Acadia's Mount Desert Island to the depths of the Virgin River where it cuts through Zion Canyon, *American Wilderness: The National Parks* offers unique and intimate portraits of nature, scenery, wildlife, and history. Included are the geothermal features of Yellowstone; mist-veiled ridges stretching to the horizon in the Great Smoky Mountains; more than 450 species of fauna at Big Bend, and Stronghold Table in Badlands, where Sioux Indians held the last Ghost Dance in 1890. Through the photography of Tom Bean, Craig Blacklock, Liz Hymans, David and Marc Muench, Pat O'Hara, Mike Sedam and Scott Smith, you can explore Death Valley, the lowest point in the Western Hemisphere; Mount Whitney, the highest peak in the Lower 48 states; Mauna Loa, the earth's most massive mountain, and the 2,500-year-old General Sherman Tree, the world's largest living thing. You will find these, and many other unique natural features, in *American Wilderness: The National Parks.*

Our journey starts with a trip back in time, to look at the origins of national parks, and see how early travelers experienced America's "wonderlands." The story begins in the 1840s, when frontier traditions and the myth of America as a second Eden inspired many to feel a sense of belonging in nature. Love of nature grew as more became known about the dramatic landscapes of the American West. Publication of John C. Frémont's *Report of the Exploring Expedition to the Rocky Mountains in the Year 1842, and to Oregon and North California in the Years 1843-1844,* and the Pacific Railroad Surveys of 1853, influenced such artists as Asher Durand and other painters of the Hudson River School. As wilderness receded before expanding civilization, wild scenery as an artistic genre attracted art patrons. Many concluded that America's greatness was best expressed through images of the sublime, a term that increasingly referred to the "wild" in nature. Rather than focusing on manmade works to give meaning to a scene, Romantic artists rendered exceptional features of the landscape in precise detail and glowing illumination, expressing nature's beauty as the direct countenance of God.

Literary figures also asserted that nature could draw humans closer to the divine. In his essay "Nature" of 1836, Ralph Waldo Emerson wrote, "Standing on the bare ground—my head bathed in the blithe air, and uplifted into infinite space— my mean egotism vanishes. I become a transparent eyeball; I am nothing; I see all; the currents of the Universal Being circulate through me; I am part and parcel of God." Travel literature popularized nature appreciation in the United States, and scenic monuments became symbols of spiritual identity. Comments left by a sightseer at Niagara Falls in 1848 record public sentiment similar to that expressed by Emerson:

> The most stupendous work of Nature! The mountains, oceans, lakes and cataracts, are great specimens of the *magnificence* of God's works; but here his *beneficence* is also indicated, by the perpetual rainbow. What mind is not changed, what soul not filled with ennobling emotions, by the contemplation of such wonders? Let man behold with awe and admiration, and learn——HUMILITY.[1]

AS THE NINETEENTH CENTURY UNFOLDED, Americans turned the spiritual associations they found in nature into feelings of national identity. The Louisiana Purchase, Oregon Trail, conquest of Mexico, and California Gold Rush opened the continent for Americans. Monumental western scenery became iconic for artists, philosophers, and political leaders seeking to bolster America's cultural independence from Europe. During the dark days of the Civil War, they looked to nature, particularly sublime scenery embodied in dramatic western landscapes, to legitimate national identity and show the divine sanction of American civilization. Through photographs by Carleton Watkins and paintings by Albert Bierstadt, reproduced and sold by the thousands, Yosemite Valley became a symbol of "Manifest Destiny," the conviction among many Americans that the United States should stretch from the Atlantic to the Pacific because it was God's will.

Preservation of Yosemite Valley and the neighboring Mariposa Big Tree Grove validated the idea that America was "nature's nation." On June 30, 1864 President Abraham Lincoln signed an act transferring ownership of the two neighboring sites to the state of California. The Yosemite Grant was "segregated from the general domain of the public lands, and devoted forever to popular resort and recreation."[2] Governor Frederick F. Low placed Frederick Law Olmsted, chief architect for New York's Central Park, in charge of an eight-member commission organized to manage Yosemite. A year later Olmsted submitted a preliminary report that established a philosophy for public preservation of natural scenery based on its unique capacity to enhance human psychological, physical, and social health.

Olmsted believed that California should protect the Yosemite Grant from private interests because spectacular natural environments, offering spiritual solace and opportunities for relaxation and recreation, were good for personal health and vigor, especially that of the intellect. Natural scenery reinvigorated people, Olmsted theorized, because it aroused the attention of their minds and occupied them without purpose, thus disrupting the thought processes that relate present actions to future ends. This break relieved the stress of daily life in the modern world, increasing the nature-goer's capacity for happiness and the means of securing it. "There is little else that has this quality so purely," wrote Olmsted.[3]

Preserving Yosemite from a monopoly by individuals was not enough. Olmsted felt the grant had to be "laid open to the use of the body of the people" as a place where visitors could reconnect with a love of nature "which the Almighty has implanted in every human being." He associated nature intimately and mysteriously with moral perceptions and intuitions. Olmsted meant to preserve Yosemite exactly as he had found it, while making allowances for the necessary accommodations of visitors. He envisioned Yosemite and the Mariposa Grove as a "museum of natural science," and recognized a need to preserve the character of rock formations, trees, plants, and animals, from the "bad taste, playfulness, carelessness, or wanton destructiveness" of visitors. Olmsted wrote:

> It is but sixteen years since the Yosemite was first seen by a white man, several visitors have since made the journey of several thousands miles at large cost to see it, and notwithstanding the difficulties which now interpose, hundreds resort to it annually. Before many years, if proper facilities are offered, these hundreds will become thousands and in a century the whole number of visitors will be counted in millions. An injury to the scenery so slight that it may be unheeded by any visitor now, will be one multiplied by these millions.[4]

IN 1869 COMPLETION OF THE FIRST TRANS-continental railroad, from Omaha, Nebraska, to Sacramento, California, made the West accessible to Americans for the first time. Travel became quick, comfortable, and safe. Finally, travelers could see for themselves the scenic wonders so widely portrayed in newspapers, magazines, paintings, and photographs. Increasing national wealth, new attitudes toward leisure, and steady reductions in costs made vacation travel possible. The outbreak of the Franco-Prussian War in 1870 discouraged Americans from European travel, and many instead decided to visit the West. Railroad promoters did everything they could to make sure eager tourists found just what they had hoped to find in the scenery. Not everyone could afford this experience. In the 1870s a trip to

L. Prang and Co. after Thomas Moran, Hot Springs of Gardiner's River, Yellowstone, 1875 (Courtesy of the Library of Congress)

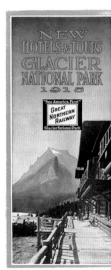

Atchison, Topeka & Santa Fe Railway tourist guide featuring horseback riding at Grand Canyon National Park, 1932 (Courtesy of the Autry Museum of Western Heritage, Los Angeles)

F. F. Palmer, Yosemite Valley—California: "The Bridal Veil," 1866 (Courtesy of the Library of Congress)

California and back from New York or Boston could take more than a month and cost $1,200. Only the wealthiest and most leisured tourists had the time and money necessary to make the trip.

Boosters were selling guidebooks before the first train rolled down the Union Pacific tracks. George A. Crofutt may have written the first one, eventually selling nearly 350,000 copies of his *Transcontinental Tourist Guide* in the 1870s. Tourists expected to be awed, thrilled, excited, and most of all entertained. Guidebooks publicized western railroad travel with a well-crafted panorama, with beautiful scenery and exciting tableaux passing constantly before the audience. Promoters did their best to describe spectacular scenery for those with money to spend on travel. Yellowstone National Park became a main attraction, described in *The Pacific Tourist* as a hunter's paradise where "Elk, deer, antelope, and smaller game are found in profusion; and all the streams and lakes abound in fish." The guidebook offered artists and nature lovers

> combinations of beauty in grand panoramas and magnificent landscapes, that are seldom equaled elsewhere. Snow-capped mountains tower grandly above the valley, seeming to pierce the clouds; while at their feet are streams, that now plunge into the depths of dark and profound canyons, and anon emerge into lovely meadow-like valleys through which they wind in graceful curves; often expanding into noble lakes with pine fringed shores, or breaking into picturesque falls and rapids.[5]

IN YELLOWSTONE, FREDERICK LAW OLMSTED'S theories about the benefits of spectacular scenery dovetailed with an understanding that American progress might irrevocably transform this Arcadian

Carleton Watkins, Yosemite Falls, 1866 (Courtesy of the Library of Congress)

paradise into a manmade wilderness. Jay Cooke, head of the Northern Pacific Railroad, promoted the idea of establishing Yellowstone as America's first national park to interest investors in subsidizing construction of his line from Minneapolis, Minnesota, to Tacoma, Washington. In 1870 Cooke hired Nathaniel P. "National Park" Langford to pen articles about his explorations of Yellowstone and give a series of lectures in Washington, New York, and Philadelphia. Langford is quoted by Hiram Chittenden in *The Yellowstone National Park* stating:

> This is probably the most remarkable region of natural wonders in the world; and, while we already have our Niagara and Yosemite, this new field of wonders should be at once withdrawn from occupancy, and set aside as a public National Park for the enjoyment of the American people for all time.[6]

Langford, however, was not the first person to put forth the idea of establishing Yellowstone National Park. That honor belongs to Judge William D. Kelly, who made the suggestion to Jay Cooke's agent, A.B. Nettleton. In turn, Nettleton proposed the idea in a letter to Ferdinand V. Hayden, Chief Geologist with the United States Geological Survey. Hayden's survey of the Yellowstone in 1871 was the first definitive exploration of the region. The survey included topographers and botanists, a meteorologist, mineralogist, agricultural statistician, and entomologist. The notable photographer William H. Jackson was also part of the Hayden Survey, along with the artist Thomas Moran, whose expenses were paid by the Northern Pacific Railroad.

Returning to Washington, Hayden arranged for geological specimens to be displayed with Jackson photographs and Moran sketches in the rotunda of the Capitol. Members of Congress received copies of official exploration reports and Langford's article "The Wonders of the Yellowstone" published in *Scribner's Monthly*. In another *Scribner's Monthly* article, "Wonder of the West — II; More about the Yellowstone," Hayden asked, "Why will not Congress at once pass a law setting it [the Yellowstone] apart as a great public park for all time to come as has been done with that far inferior wonder, the Yosemite Valley?"[7]

On March 1, 1872 President Ulysses S. Grant established the first national park by signing an act setting apart "a certain Tract of Land lying near the Head-waters of the Yellowstone River as...a public park or pleasureing-ground for the benefit and enjoyment of the people."[8] The railroads spared no expense promoting

Yellowstone as a tourist destination. Chromolithographs, colorfully written and illustrated guidebooks, stereograph cards, and postcards acquainted tourists and would-be tourists alike with America's first national park. Subjects for these popular mediums included railroads and accommodations as well as the park's natural attractions.

Access to Yellowstone National Park was difficult in the early days. The only option was a dusty, bumpy carriage ride from Virginia City or Bozeman, Montana. Circumstances changed in 1883, when the Northern Pacific Railroad completed a branch line from Livingston to Cinnabar, Montana. Northern Pacific shareholders formed the Yellowstone Park Improvement Company and hired St. Paul architect L. F. Buffington to design the Queen Anne-style National Hotel. Built to house 800 guests, the hotel was situated at Mammoth Hot Springs because it was the main attraction closest to Cinnabar.

Guides hauled passengers from the railroad depot to the hotel and on through the park. They offered a "Grand Tour" of Yellowstone that recalled European travel, but featured volcanic geysers and hot springs, instead of stately cathedrals and ancient castles. In 1884 tent hotels operated by William Wallace Wylie offered cheaper, less luxuriant accommodations for rugged sightseers wanting to view Yellowstone the "Wylie Way." Early tourists took advantage of bathhouses in the geyser basins. Sporting sightseers descended into the Grand Canyon of the Yellowstone, as the chasm carved by the river became known, on horseback. Bear-feeding was another attraction, one that quickly led to problems.

In 1903 the Yellowstone Park Association (successor to the Yellowstone Park Improvement Company) chose Seattle architect Robert Reamer to design and build the Old Faithful Inn. This new hotel within the Upper Geyser Basin served tourists entering Yellowstone from the west. By 1908 the Union Pacific Railroad brought sightseers to the "gateway community" of West Yellowstone. Later, the Burlington line reached Cody, Wyoming, and from there tourists traveled by bus to Yellowstone's east entrance.

By 1910 lobbying and support from six transcontinental railroad companies led to the creation of eight national parks. California was home to three new parks established in 1890: Sequoia, General Grant (made part of Kings Canyon National Park in 1940), and Yosemite. John Muir convincingly argued that the state of California could not save Yosemite Valley, the mile-wide, seven-mile-long canyon that occupies only 1 percent of the present-day park, without protection for its Sierra

fountains, the mountain peaks, high country meadows, and ancient forests where waters gathered before rushing over valley waterfalls. In 1906 California gave up Yosemite Valley and it was incorporated into Yosemite National Park. The next season, Southern Pacific travelers could leave the main line at Merced and ride the Yosemite Valley Railway to the gateway of El Portal. The Southern Pacific Railroad worked hard to promote Yosemite as a destination for tourists. Sequoia, Grant Grove, and Kings Canyon remained less accessible and consequently received fewer visitors.

In the Pacific Northwest, Mount Rainier gained national park status in 1899. The Northern Pacific promoted Mount Rainier, an immense volcanic dome rising 14,410 feet, near Seattle, Washington, for years through its *Wonderland* series of guidebooks. It was the Chicago, Milwaukee & Puget Sound Railway, however, through its Tacoma Eastern subsidiary, that developed the park. Mountain climbing was the main attraction for such tourists as Joseph Hazard, who wrote,

> In trail work the real mountain man does not climb to get somewhere—he climbs to be on the way. In climbing to the summit of Mount Rainier we lift two days out of prosaic existence. We enter a world of the unreal, a realm of the ideal, where all dross is refined away. We climb upward hour by hour while our spirit soars to meet ever-changing vistas and ever-widening panoramic reaches.[9]

Crater Lake, twenty-one square miles of intensely blue water cradled in an extinct volcano in southern Oregon, became America's sixth national park in 1902. The Southern Pacific Railroad, in particular, publicized Crater Lake as a destination. The seventh park to be designated, Wind Cave, South Dakota, established by President Theodore Roosevelt in 1903, was the first one created to protect a cave.

In 1906 Congress passed "An act for the preservation of American antiquities," authorizing the President to establish national monuments to preserve features of historical, prehistoric, and scientific interest. The American Antiquities Act linked preservation of cultural resources with that of natural resources (an association that would allow the Carter administration to halt construction of the Trans-Alaska pipeline pending resolution of Native peoples' land claims). It gave President Theodore Roosevelt power to create national monuments on his own initiative.

Mesa Verde, which preserves thousands of prehistoric sites, including multistoried cliff dwellings built into rock alcoves above

Dr. J. Walter Fewkes, Chief of the Bureau of American Ethnology, from "The Prehistoric Cliff Dwellings of Mesa Verde National Park, Colorado," about 1920 (Courtesy of the Autry Museum of Western Heritage, Los Angeles)

the Montezuma Valley of southern Colorado, was the first National Park created "specifically for the preservation from injury or spoliation of the ruins and other works and relics of prehistoric or primitive man."[10] The Secretary of the Interior authorized legitimate investigations of the ruins by properly qualified and affiliated archaeologists, such as Dr. J. Walter Fewkes from the Smithsonian Institution. Fewkes and other archaeologists at Mesa Verde helped interpret the ruins and the "Cliff Dwellers" who had lived there for groups touring the park. In *Our Trip to Mesa Verde*, Ruth Miller describes meeting Dr. Fewkes: "Just before we arrived they had unearthed eight pieces of pottery, corn, feathers, cloth, implements, skulls, other bones, etc. Dr. Fewkes told us all about the things and then climbed to the top of the wall to have his picture taken."[11]

Protecting the remains of prehistoric cultures in Mesa Verde National Park provided Americans with a history they could use for their own cultural needs. The ancient ruins supplied a link to the past that was

William Henry Jackson, U.S. Geological Survey pack train on trail along the Yellowstone River, 1871 (Courtesy of the Library of Congress)

Unknown photographer, Stephen T. Mather, 1920s (Courtesy of the Library of Congress)

based in the New World, instead of Europe. Likewise, Native Americans living in the Southwest also established New World connections: Hopi, Navajo, and Pueblo peoples offered clues for living without the trappings of modern life. New research and writings by ethnologists and archaeologists offered more justifications for the active protection of nature. Modern people could not rejuvenate themselves, following Indian examples of wilderness living, if no wilderness existed. Environmental protection of wilderness areas became a new focus of sporting groups like the Appalachian Mountain Club, Boone and Crocket Club, Sierra Club, and Mazamas of Oregon.

The Atchison, Topeka & Santa Fe Railway responded quickly to public interest in Native peoples. Between 1896 and 1920, the Santa Fe built seventeen large hotels and an equal number of station depots boasting "mission-style" architecture. With the Fred Harvey Company as a partner, the railroad invented southwestern adventures for the touring public. They incorporated the cultures, values, and images of Native Americans from New Mexico and Arizona into a travel experience that emphasized good food, clean rooms, and excellent "Harvey Girl" service. They promoted the Southwest as an "Indian Detour" en route from Chicago to Los Angeles, with the Grand Canyon of the Colorado in northern Arizona as a main attraction.

One of the most spectacular examples of erosion anywhere in the world, the Grand Canyon offered visitors incomparable vistas. Though the Grand Canyon did not become a national park until 1919, the Santa Fe Railway began extensive promotion of it as a tourist destination soon after a branch line was opened in 1901 from Williams, Arizona, to the

south rim. The railroad hired Charles Whittlesey to design the spectacular El Tovar Hotel, combining qualities of a Swiss chalet and a Norwegian villa, with interiors representing a wide range of styles and periods. By the time El Tovar opened in 1905, the Fred Harvey Company had packaged a tourist experience that combined easy access and luxurious accommodations with great scenery and exotic history.

Across from El Tovar, Fred Harvey architect Mary Jane Colter designed and decorated Hopi House to feature Native craftspeople living and working in harmony with the Grand Canyon. Colter modeled the building after one in the Hopi village of Old Oraibi. It was intended to be a place where tourists could watch Native Americans dance, weave blankets, hammer silver, fire pottery, cook meals, and carry on other activities of daily life. Entertaining and educational, *El Tovar, Grand Canyon of Arizona* describes Hopi House:

Several rooms in the Hopi House are devoted to an exhibit of rare and costly specimens of Indian and Mexican handiwork. Here is displayed the priceless Harvey collection of old Navajo blankets, winner of a grand prize at the Louisiana Purchase Exposition; and finally, a salesroom containing the most interesting display of genuine Indian and Mexican handiwork in this country, gathered from all sections of the Southwest and Northwest.[12]

H OPI HOUSE WAS PIVOTAL IN THE FRED Harvey Company's plan to create and grow markets for Southwestern Indian arts and crafts. The theme of Native Americans in harmony with nature was extended along the entire south rim of the Grand Canyon through a series of Colter-designed scenic viewpoints: Lookout Studio (1914), Hermit's Rest (1914), Desert

Photograph by Allan Rinehart, Acadia National Park, Maine, 1934 (Courtesy of the National Park Service)

View Watchtower (1932), and Bright Angel Lodge (1935).

Not to be outdone, Louis W. Hill incorporated elements of Blackfeet culture into tourist facilities, programs, and marketing plans developed by the Great Northern Railway for Glacier, Montana. As president of the Great Northern, Hill helped create Glacier National Park in 1910, because its hundreds of lakes, dozens of glaciers, and abrupt alpine peaks afforded a perfect destination for his rail passengers. Hill hired the artist Wienold Reiss to produce artwork using images of Blackfeet Indians to feature in the Great Northern's advertising campaigns touting "See America First" and "The National Park Route."

Hill knew the Great Northern's wealthy clientele demanded exceptional accommodations. In response, he opened Glacier Park Lodge in 1913. This sensational lodge became the gateway to Glacier for travelers coming from the east. By the end of 1914 Hill opened Many Glacier Hotel on the shores of Swiftcurrent Lake. A series of remote chalets, accessible only by boat or trail, linked these two log palaces.

For many, the trip from Glacier Park Lodge to Many Glacier Hotel became the ultimate backcountry adventure. Mary Roberts Rinehart captured the essence of her 1913 trip in her book *Through Glacier Park*: "With the second day came a new sense of physical well-being, and this in spite of a sunburn that had swollen my face like a toothache. Already the telephones and invitations to dinner and tailor's fittings and face powder belonged to the forgotten past."[13] Upon completing her trip, Rinehart was comforted when, "At Glacier Park station my wardrobe, which I had not seen in weeks, was put on the train. 'They do you very well,' as the English say, in the West. Everything was pressed. Even my shoes had been freshly polished."[14] In 1927 Louis Hill completed his last project, the Prince of Wales Hotel located in the neighboring Waterton National Park of Alberta, Canada. The existence of equivalent luxury accommodations on both sides of the border facilitated combination of the two parks into Waterton-Glacier International Peace Park in 1932.

While Louis Hill was busy developing tourist attractions in Glacier, John Muir and other preservationists were trying to save the Hetch Hetchy Valley, protected in Yosemite National Park, from being dammed as a reservoir to provide water for San Francisco. The campaign to save Hetch Hetchy, chronicled in the national press, received the attention of conservationists across the country. The debate over dam construction signaled an ideological split within the conservation movement between preservationists, seeking to retain public preserves in their natural state, and utilitarians, who advocated sustainable harvesting of natural resources for human benefit. The controversy is typified by writings such as John Muir's "Let Everyone Help to Save the Famous Hetch Hetchy Valley and Stop the Commercial Destruction Which Threatens Our National Parks" (1911) and "Water and Power for San Francisco from Hetch Hetchy Valley in Yosemite National Park" by Martin Vilas (1915).[15] Congress passed the Raker Act granting San

Francisco permission to dam Hetch Hetchy, and President Woodrow Wilson signed the bill on December 19, 1913. Though a major defeat for preservationists, debate over Hetch Hetchy hastened the movement to maturity. Park preservation gained a new level of awareness and importance in national life. The loss of Hetch Hetchy galvanized campaigns to create an independent federal bureau to protect and care for national parks.

In 1916 Congress passed the National Park Service Act, creating the National Park Service within the Department of the Interior. This landmark legislation incorporated forty years of thinking, since the establishment of Yellowstone National Park, into an agency dedicated to park stewardship. The mission of the National Park Service was defined as:

promote and regulate the use of the Federal areas known as national parks, monuments, and reservations...by such means and measures as conform to the fundamental purpose of the said parks, monuments, and reservations, which purpose is to conserve the scenery and the natural and historic objects and the wild life therein and to provide for the enjoyment of the same in such manner and by such means as will leave them unimpaired for the enjoyment of future generations.[16]

Unknown photographer, Record Group 79, Bear-feeding show at Yellowstone National Park, 1920s (Courtesy of the National Archives and Records Administration, Yellowstone National Park)

S TEPHEN T. MATHER WAS RECRUITED TO HEAD the National Park Service. A Chicago businessman and University of California graduate, by 1914 Mather had made a small fortune selling borax. As pictured by biographer Robert Shankland, Mather was "at the pinnacle of success, forty-seven years old, an enormously personable, energetic, and hard-driving man, who was a trifle restless and on the lookout for new worlds to conquer."[17] As its first director, Mather set goals for the National Park Service (NPS) that aimed to build public support for parks. Congress was unwilling to appropriate significant funds for park preservation without evidence of public support, and increasing

Jack Timeche with a customer in the Watchtower gift shop, Grand Canyon National Park, 1930s (Courtesy of Grand Canyon National Park)

visitation seemed the best way to convince the Congress to fund the National Park Service. Toward this end, Mather advocated resource development of a different type: building new tourist accommodations and improving existing facilities, coupled with road construction to permit a larger number of people to reach the parks. The inherent contradiction found in promoting tourism while attempting to preserve nature in national parks was not lost on many preservationists.

To generate more publicity and promote the parks, Mather turned to friends working for eastern newspapers and editors of leading magazines. He persuaded Robert Sterling Yard to give up his job as an editor of the *New York Herald* to head a NPS information office. Yard produced a collection of pamphlets, which were released as the *National Parks Portfolio*, that advertised the parks as "America's Playgrounds" and targeted an audience who could afford both to travel and to support national parks. Mather induced such writers as novelist Emerson Hough to pen articles for *Saturday Evening Post* and other leading magazines. Gilbert Grosvenor, editor of *National Geographic*, dedicated most of the April 1916 issue to national parks. A chain of Midwestern newspapers, owned by a friend in Chicago, ran a series of articles.

Despite opposition from some preservationists, Mather believed that national parks needed more and better roads and new tourist facilities. World War I had stemmed the tide of European travel, and he took advantage of that disruption to encourage sightseers to "See America First." In Denver, Mather promoted a new National Park-to-Park Highway Association, organized to build a 3,500-mile road linking national parks in the Rockies, North Cascade, Olympic, and Sierra mountain ranges. When Interior Secretary Franklin Lane first authorized the admission of private automobiles to Yellowstone in 1915, Americans immediately began discovering the joys of automobile touring in national parks. Their enthusiasm was sufficient to reorient all existing park developments: new facilities and services, like auto camps and gas stations, were added to the landscape.

Earl E. Evans for Record Group 79, Cars in the parking area for the Canyon bear-feeding show on Otter Creek in Yellowstone National Park, 1935 (Courtesy of the National Archives and Records Administration, Yellowstone National Park)

Unknown Photographer, Climbers on Tyndall Glacier in Rocky Mountain National Park, 1916 (Courtesy of the National Park Service)

Unknown photographer, Phantom Ranch, designed by Mary Jane Colter, on Bright Angel Creek at the bottom of the Grand Canyon of Arizona, 1932 (Courtesy of the Autry Museum of Western Heritage, Los Angeles)

The automobile gave tourists the geographic range of the railroad without restricting them to fixed routes and rigid schedules. Automobile tourists could go when and where they wanted at their own speed.

Mather felt that making national parks accessible to automobile tourism would increase visitation, which he needed to secure the future of all parks. As the NPS built roads and expanded roadside services during the 1920s, parks became accessible to many middle-class Americans for the first time. Visitations increased from 356,097 in 1916, to 2,774,561 in 1930.[18] These new tourists, like the smaller group in the earlier era, responded to the spiritual values of nature and felt a reinvigorated sense of American identity, which they associated with national parks. Traveling by car along national highways, auto-tourists attempted to relive American frontier history and pioneer experiences. In a world before motels and fast-food restaurants, these "sagebrushers" traveled independently, camping in open areas along the side of the road. Many became ardent supporters of wilderness preservation.

As visitation grew, Congress increased funding for national parks and created new parks including Rocky

Mountain, Colorado (1915), Hawaii (1916), Lassen Volcanic, California (1916), Mount McKinley, Alaska (1917; incorporated into Denali, 1980), Grand Canyon, Arizona (1919), Zion, Utah (1919), Hot Springs, Arkansas (1921), and Bryce Canyon, Utah (1928). These new parks gave Americans more places to visit, induced development, and brought much-needed tourist dollars into remote and sparsely populated regions.

Automobile tourists were typically born westerners or transplanted easterners, who lived in and around growing cities like Los Angeles, Seattle, and Phoenix. They enjoyed active, outdoor lifestyles and helped transform recreation into daily exercise. They visited parks like Yosemite, Mount Rainier, and Grand Canyon during two-week summer vacations—without having to take long, expensive, cross-country train trips. For many, auto-touring in national parks became an annual rite of passage. While "doing the national parks," auto-tourists brought a new emphasis on outdoor recreation to "America's Playgrounds." As camping, hiking, climbing, fishing, backpacking, horseback riding, skiing, and river running caught on quickly, outdoor fun began to overshadow the more passive social and psychological

enjoyments of earlier generations. By the 1920s, road trips and family camping in national parks were on their way to becoming American institutions.

The Rockefellers, Morgans, Fords, Vanderbilts, Carnegies, and Astors, who spent summers on Mount Desert Island in Maine, assisted Mather in his efforts to establish the first national park in the East. George B. Dorr, head of the Hancock County Trustees of Public Reservations, aided Mather's efforts by donating 6,000 acres of Mount Desert to the federal government. Dorr continued to acquire property hoping to obtain full national park status for the island even after President Wilson signed the bill creating Sieur de Monts National Monument. Finally, in 1919 Wilson announced the establishment of Lafayette National Park, the first national park east of the Mississippi River. Dorr, considered "the greatest of one-man show in the history of land conservation," became the first park superintendent. In 1929 the park name changed to Acadia.[19]

To attract more tourists to the park system, Mather planned to create additional parks east of the Mississippi that were easily accessible by automobile from Boston, New York, Philadelphia, and other urban centers. East Coast auto-tourists would increase overall park-use statistics, thereby building more support in Congress for all national park preservation. He began preservation efforts in the Great Smoky Mountains of North Carolina and Tennessee, Shenandoah, Virginia, Mammoth Cave, Kentucky, and Everglades, Florida; however, several years passed before Congress cooperated in establishing these parks.

In January 1929, Horace Albright, Stephen Mather's longtime assistant, was sworn in as the second director of the National Park Service. Albright sought to consolidate gains and strengthen protection within the National Park Service for all the new parks established since 1916. He recommended extending boundaries in some parks and oversaw the establishment of three new parks—Grand Teton, Wyoming (1929), Carlsbad Caverns, New Mexico (1930), and Isle Royale, Michigan (1931). Albright convinced President Franklin D. Roosevelt to transfer to the National Park Service,

historical monuments, battlefields, memorials, and historic sites administered by the War Department and other federal agencies. All totaled, the National Park Service gained forty-eight units, plus nearly seven hundred buildings in the District of Columbia. Roosevelt's executive order put the NPS in charge of administration for historical and archaeological sites and structures all over the country. As the Park Service expanded its influence, the bureau grew strong enough to resist further attempts to merge it with other agencies.

After 1933, Albright's successor, Arno Cammerer, found work for millions of unemployed young men, who left cities and towns across America to join the Civilian Conservation Corps (CCC). From 1933 to 1942, the CCC introduced many working-class Americans representing every race, ethnicity, and region of the country to national parks for the first time. The CCC provided manpower and materials to build shelters, picnic areas, campgrounds, swimming pools, foot trails, scenic overlooks, and other recreational facilities in national parks. Crews built water and sewage systems, stocked fish, restored historic buildings, assembled museums, constructed roads and bridges, planted trees, curbed erosion, and controlled mosquitoes. In 1935 more than 500 camps were at work on NPS projects. During its nine-year existence the CCC accomplished tasks that would otherwise have taken fifty years to complete.

Designs for tourist facilities built by CCC workers emphasized mass recreation and automobile touring. In World's Work, for example, Horace Kephart describes a thirty-five-mile "skyline highway" proposed from Indian Gap to the Tennessee River in Great Smoky Mountains:

From many points on the skyline road there will be vistas of a hundred miles out over the Appalachian Valley to the blue Cumberlands on the western horizon, while to the eastward the visitors will behold a sea of wooded mountains as far as the eye can reach. At times the touring parties will be above the clouds; at times they may witness the strange phenomena of thunderstorms or rainbows far below them in the mountain gulfs.[20]

CONGRESS ESTABLISHED FIVE NEW PARKS during this period—Great Smoky Mountains, North Carolina and Tennessee (1934), Shenandoah, Virginia (1935), Olympic, Washington (1938), Kings Canyon, California (1940), and Mammoth Cave, Kentucky (1941)—but commercial opportunism, fueled by American involvement in World War II, threatened many national parks. Timber interests tried unsuccessfully to gain access to old-growth forests in Olympic National Park. William Greeley, head of the West Coast Lumbermen's Association, made an eloquent and passionate appeal for the industry in 1943 when he wrote: "The Olympic Peninsula National Park [sic] should do its part towards victory by giving up certain of its fine grade, old growth timber to the war effort. The principle of the draft should extend from our boys to our resources. Nothing is too sacred to do its share."[21] California stockmen petitioned the National Park Service for grazing rights in Sequoia. However, Newton Drury, its newly appointed director, successfully launched widely publicized campaigns of radio addresses and articles to portray these efforts as shortsighted and opportunistic rather than patriotic. The only new park added to the system during World War II was Big Bend (1944), in the Chihuahuan Desert of west Texas, where the Rio Grande cuts between the southern Rocky Mountains and Mexico's Sierra Madre Mountains.

When wartime restrictions on travel were lifted, veterans, many of them former CCC workers, returned to national parks in droves. With families in tow, these middle- and working-class Americans numbered among the most avid park supporters. The newly created Everglades National Park (1947) on the southernmost tip of Florida was a popular destination. The February 1948 issue of Popular Mechanics described Everglades as "Uncle Sam's Jungle Playground":

The aim of the park staff is to maintain the 'Glades as a wilderness and to keep the wildlife undisturbed in its natural surroundings. For that reason road building will be kept to a minimum. But you will be able to see the park on conducted tours by boat and on foot...The Seminole Indians once fought a war with the United

Unknown photographer, Visitors wading in the warm water flowing from Great Fountain Geyser in Yellowstone National Park, before 1915 (Courtesy of the Yellowstone National Park Museum Record Group 79)

"The Wonders of Geyserland," the cover illustration for a portfolio of images entitled "The Grand Tour of Yellowstone National Park," 1913 (Courtesy of the Autry Museum of Western Heritage, Los Angeles)

Photograph by Hileman, Interior view of Glacier Park Lodge, Glacier National Park, 1913 (Courtesy of Glacier National Park)

States and then retreated deep into the Everglades without signing a peace treaty. The park plans to establish a Seminole camp accessible to tourists, but no attempt will be made to lure large numbers of Indians back to the park...Facilities for tourists are limited but eventually...[t]here'll be museums, roadside displays and lectures in addition to escorted tours.[22]

Hundreds of war-trained aviators wanted to fly small planes over Grand Canyon, Yellowstone, and other parks during their summer vacations. Anticipating that air travel would one day be common, Assistant Interior Secretary Girard Davidson championed construction of gateway airports in the July 1949 issue of *Flying*: "Locating airports just outside park boundaries would...follow the precedent set by the National Park Service in its treatment of the railroads....The resulting volume of air traffic would encourage the development of related hotels, restaurants

George A. Grant, Lunch time in Piegan Pass, Glacier National Park, 1932 (Courtesy of the National Park Service)

and other businesses in connection with the airport."[23]

During the 1950s, in the postwar climate of unbridled enthusiasm for economic development, NPS director Conrad Wirth launched a scheme called "Mission 66" to build accommodations and, consequently, huge increases in visitation. In time for its fiftieth anniversary in 1966, the National Park Service set out once again to build public support by expanding the range of park uses. Mission 66 rebuilt existing park roads and constructed new ones, built and improved trails, campgrounds, picnic areas, parking lots, campfire circles, amphitheaters, and comfort stations. A hallmark of Mission 66 was the park visitor center, a multiuse amenity with interpretive exhibits, audiovisual programs, and public services.

In *Desert Solitaire*, naturalist Edward Abbey, who worked for the Park Service at Arches National Monument in Utah, offered his appraisal of Mission 66, coining the term "Industrial Tourism" to describe the results:

> The little campgrounds...have now been consolidated into one master campground that looks, during the busy season, like a suburban village: elaborate housetrailers of quilted aluminum crowd upon gigantic camper-trucks of Fiberglas and molded plastic; through their windows you will see the blue glow of television and hear the studio laughter of Los Angeles; knobby-kneed oldsters in plaid Bermudas buzz up and down the quaintly curving asphalt road on motorbikes; quarrels break out between campsite neighbors while others gather around their burning charcoal briquettes...to compare electric toothbrushes. The Comfort Stations are there, too, all lit up with electricity, fully equipped inside, though the generator breaks down now and then and the lights go out, or the sewage backs up in the plumbing system...and the water supply sometimes fails...Down at the beginning of the new road, at park headquarters, is the new entrance station and visitor center, where admission fees are collected and where the rangers are going quietly nuts answering the same three basic questions five hundred times a day: (1) Where's the john? (2) How long's it take to see this place? (3) Where's the Coke machine?[24]

Developing more and better tourist facilities, and more parks—Virgin Islands (1956), Haleakala (1960, split from Hawaii), Petrified Forest, Arizona (1962), and Canyonlands, Utah (1964)—inevitably led more people to visit. By 1974 visitations climbed to forty-six million, more than three times the fourteen million tourists visiting national parks in 1955.[25] In the wake of this growth, and the publicity surrounding new recreational opportunities, areas in many national parks seemed to lose their meditative and rejuvenating qualities. No longer refuges from urbanization, many parks lost the intimacy and mystery that originally veiled them, becoming choked by traffic jams, blaring horns, noxious fumes, and smog. Bottles, cans, and paper littering the ground despoiled the landscape; the freedom of individual cars now made people who suffered in traffic tense and grumpy. Overdevelopment began to crowd primary preservation goals.

Sensitivity to the environmental and aesthetic consequences of park development increased after 1963, when Interior Secretary Stewart Udall's Advisory Board on Wildlife Management published the now-famous Leopold

Unknown photographer, The El Tovar Hotel viewed from Hopi House, Grand Canyon National Park, ca. 1910 (Courtesy of the Autry Museum of Western Heritage, Los Angeles)

Lobby of the Old Faithful Inn, Yellowstone National Park, after 1904 (Courtesy of the Montana Historical Society)

Report. Chaired by wildlife biologist A. Starker Leopold, the Board argued that increased automobile tourism, considered a salvation by Stephen Mather in 1916, now threatened preservation. The Leopold Report called for historical and ecological research to develop new skills needed to manage natural resources. It recommended protecting roadless wilderness areas from future development and urged the removal of recreational amenities that compromised park values such as golf courses, ski lifts, and motorboat marinas. "As a primary goal we would recommend that the biotic associations within each park be maintained, or where necessary recreated, as nearly as possible in the condition that prevailed when the area was first visited by the white men...A national park should represent a vignette of primitive America."[26]

New legislation encouraged more and greater efforts towards preservation. The Wilderness Act of 1964, National Historic Preservation Act of 1966, National Trails System Act of 1968, and Wild and Scenic Rivers Act of 1968 established new unit designations within the NPS. New areas for recreation like Ozark National Scenic Riverways in Missouri and the Appalachian National Scenic Trail, running 2,000 miles from Maine to Georgia, helped relieve some pressure from overcrowding in national parks.

After 1972 National Recreation Areas near urban centers including Gateway (New York), Golden Gate (San Francisco), Cuyahoga Valley (Cleveland), Chattahoochee River (Atlanta), and Santa Monica Mountains (Los Angeles) provided more relief for national parks. So did the eight new parks created between 1968 and 1978: North Cascades, Washington (1968), Redwood, California (1968), Arches, Utah (1971), Capitol Reef, Utah (1971), Guadalupe Mountains, Texas (1972), Voyageurs, Minnesota (1975), Badlands, South Dakota (1978), and Theodore Roosevelt, North Dakota (1978).

By 1976 *National Parks & Conservation Magazine* was championing propane-powered shuttle buses as "Alternatives to the Auto," and condemning snowmobiles for being noisy and conflicting with park values. *Sunset* published an

article charting "Ways to reach the national parks of the West without using your car." Once inside, the magazine suggested several ways for tourists to get around. "You can get to most of the scenic attractions, visitor centers, ranger-guided walks, campfire programs, and other interpretive services by using a shuttle bus, renting a bicycle, walking, or taking a commercial bus, boat, jeep, or horseback tour operating in the park."[27]

Environmental education, featuring special programs for children, became the cornerstone of National Park Service interpretive programs. Ecology increased public understanding of the world and its life. Interpretive programs stressed how survival, and the health of the

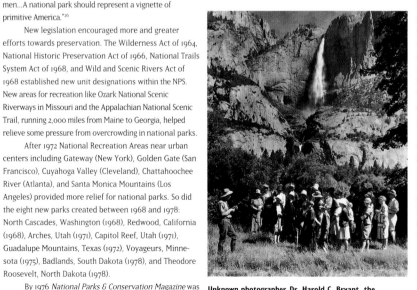

Unknown photographer, Dr. Harold C. Bryant, the "father" of National Park Service interpretation, leads a nature walk in Yosemite National Park, 1920s (Courtesy of the National Park Service)

planet, depended on ecological relationships throughout the world. Parks became learning laboratories where ecologists studied the organization of the natural world on three main levels: populations, communities, and ecosystems. Public interest in national parks began shifting from scenery to science. With visitor totals in the millions, park interpreters took advantage of new technologies for mass communications in their efforts to help park-goers learn about nature. Articles in special interest magazines as diverse as *Ebony* and *Seventeen* echoed the curiosity about ecology and reflected increasing civic awareness of environmental politics.

In 1980 Congress established national parks at Channel Islands, California, and Biscayne, Florida, before passing the mammoth Alaska National Interest Lands Conservation Act (ANILCA), which more than doubled the size of the national park system. ANILCA reserved 47 million acres of Alaska wilderness, creating eight new national parks: Denali, Gates of the Arctic, Glacier Bay, Katmai, Kenai Fjords, Kobuk Valley, Lake Clark, and Wrangell-St. Elias. "Never has so much been done on conservation for future generations with one stroke of the pen," wrote Charles Clusen, chair of the Alaska Coalition.[28]

Wrangell-St. Elias National Park encompassed more than 8,300,000 acres, with 4,900,000 additional acres set aside in the adjoining Wrangell-St. Elias National Preserve. Covering an area larger than New Hampshire and Vermont, Wrangell-St. Elias holds the greatest array of glaciers and peaks above 16,000 feet in North America. Nature writer Chip Brown described the attractions of Wrangell-St. Elias in an article titled "Alaska's Mountain Kingdom":

> We could see only wilderness far and wide in all directions, land that implied the wolf, the loon, the brown bear. We could see Dall sheep, for which the Wrangells are prized by photographers and hunters alike, scrambling agilely across the talus chutes two thousand feet above us. Ahead were only voluminous green-floored valleys and other swollen nonnego-

Poster designed by Dorothy Waugh, Life at its best:
National Parks, 1930s (Courtesy of the Montana
Historical Society)

Poster. The North Coast Limited in the Montana Rockies,
1930s (Courtesy of the Montana Historical Society)

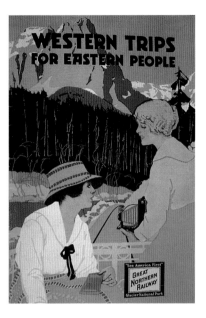

Brochure. Advertisement for the Great Northern Railway's
"See America First" campaign to lure eastern tourists to
Glacier National Park,1920s (Courtesy of the Oregon
Historical Society)

NOTES:

1 Table Rock Album and Sketches of the Falls and Scenery Adjacent (Buffalo, New York: Steam Press of Thomas & Lathrops, 1848), 39.

2 U.S. Statutes at Large, Vol. 13, Chap. 184, p. 325. "An Act authorizing a Grant to the State of California of the Yosemite Valley,' and of the Land embracing the Mariposa Big Tree Grove.'" [S. 203; Public Act No. 159] U.S. Congress. 38th. 1st Session.

3 Frederick Law Olmsted, Yosemite and the Mariposa Grove: A Preliminary Report, 1865 (Yosemite National Park, California: Yosemite ASSOCIATION,1995), 16.

4 Olmsted, Yosemite and the Mariposa Grove, 23.

5 Frederick E. Shearer, editor, The Pacific Tourist: Adams & Bishop's Illustrated Trans-Continental Guide of Travel from The Atlantic to the Pacific Ocean (New York: Adams & Bishop, 1884, reprinted by Crown Publishers, New York, 1970), 161.

6 Quoted in Aubrey L. Haines, The Yellowstone Story: A History of Our First National Park, volume one, revised edition (Yellowstone National Park, Wyoming: The Yellowstone Association for Natural Science, History & Education, 1996), 138.

7 Hayden quoted in Haines, The Yellowstone Story, volume one, 171.

8 U.S. Statutes at Large, Vol. 17, Chap. 24, pp. 32-33. "An Act to set apart a certain Tract of Land lying near the Head-waters of the Yellowstone River as a public Park." [S. 392] U.S. Congress. 42nd. 2nd Session.

9 Joseph Taylor Hazard, The Glacier Playfields of Mount Rainier National Park (Seattle: Western Printing Company, 1920), 9.

10 U.S. Statutes at Large, Vol. 34, Part 1, Chap. 3060, p. 225. "An Act For the preservation of American antiquities." [S. 4698, Public Act No. 209], U.S. Congress. 59th. 1st Session; U.S. Statutes at Large, Vol. 34, Part 1, Chap. 3607, pp. 616-17. "An Act Creating the Mesa Verde National Park." [H.R. 5998, Public Act No. 353], U.S. Congress. 59th. 1st Session.

11 Ruth Miller, Our Trip to Mesa Verde-1922 (Ouray, Colorado: Buckskin Trading Company, 1988), 21.

12 Kathleen L. Howard and Dianna F. Pardue, Inventing the Southwest: The Fred Harvey Company and Native American Art (Phoenix: The Heard Museum, 1996), 102.

13 Mary Roberts Rinehart, Through Glacier Park in 1915 (Boulder, Colorado: Roberts Rinehart Publishers, 1993), 33.

14 Rinehart, Through Glacier Park, 91.

15 Library of Congress, The Evolution of the Conservation Movement, "http://lcweb2.loc.gov/ammem/amrvhtml/cnchron4.html" (13 June 1998); Library of Congress, The Evolution of the Conservation Movement, "http://lcweb2.loc.gov/ammem/amrvhtml/cnchron6.html" (13 June 1998).

16 U.S. Statutes at Large, Vol. 39, Part 1, Chap. 408, pp. 535-36. "An Act To establish a National Park Service, and for other purposes." [H.R. 15522, Public Act No. 235], U.S. Congress. 64th. 1st Session.

17 Robert Shankland, Steve Mather of the National Parks, third edition, (New York: Alfred A. Knopf, 1970), 104, quoted in John C. Miles, Guardians of the Parks: A History of the National Parks and Conservation Association (Washington, D.C.: Taylor & Francis, 1995), 13.

18 Robert Sterling Yard, National Parks Portfolio, sixth edition (Washington, D.C.: U.S. Goverment Printing Office, 1931), 2.

19 National Park Service, "History of Acadia," in Acadia National Park Home Page, "http://www.nps.gov/acad/w95026ap.html" (13 June 1998).

20 Horace Kephart, "The Last of the Eastern Wilderness," World's Work (April 1926), 624.

21 Seattle Post-Intelligencer (June 9, 1943), quoted in Miles, Guardians of the Parks, 139.

22 "Uncle Sam's Jungle Playgrounds," Popular Mechanics (February 1948), 118-119.

23 C. Girard Davidson, "Let's Build Airports for the National Parks," Flying (July 1949), 15.

24 Edward Abbey, Desert Solitaire: A Season in the Wilderness (New York: Ballantine Books, 1968), 51-52.

25 Alfred Runte, National Parks: The American Experience, revised second edition (Lincoln and London: University of Nebraska Press, 1987), 173.

26 Miles, Guardians of the Parks, 221-222.

27 "Ways to reach the national parks of the West without using your car," Sunset (July 1979).

28 Quoted in Runte, National Parks, 255.

29 Chip Brown, "Wrangell-St. Elias: Alaska's Mountain Kingdom," National Parks & Conservation Magazine 52 (August 1978), 4.

Northern Pacific Railway tourist guide
featuring Yellowstone Falls in Yellowstone
National Park, 1910 (Courtesy of the Autry
Museum of Western Heritage, Los Angeles)

tiable creeks. Farther south lay immense broad-backed glaciers, ice fields, and mountains sometimes called "the Jewels of Alaska."[29]

Greater emphasis on recreation resulted in unprecedented numbers of tourists. "Day trippers" surpassed overnight visitors. Demand for recreational opportunities was influenced by changing patterns of land use: housing tracts replaced rural farmlands; gateway communities filled up with recent transplants. Commitment to fitness inspired many baby-boomers to try such physically demanding, high-risk adventures as rock climbing and white water sports. Technological changes in recreation equipment made these activities and others easier and more comfortable. By 1984 American consumers were spending $100 billion on outdoor recreation.

In 1990 more than 58 million people visited national parks. A report entitled A Diversity of Visitors profiled park use, showing that people of all ages visit, but families are the most common groups. Tourists represent a global community: in parks like Grand Canyon, foreign visitors sometimes outnumber Americans. Increased prosperity in some nations and maturation of the tourism industry worldwide have led more foreign tourists to include visiting national parks on their "see America" itineraries. Such factors as costs, access, facilities, and the natural features of each park influence rates of visitation across the system. Tourists list sightseeing, camping, and touring as the purpose of their visits and report that they appreciate park maps, good directional signs, and clean restrooms. The

growth of the park system continues with the recent addition of five new destinations: American Samoa (1988), Dry Tortugas, Florida (1992), Death Valley, California (1994), Joshua Tree, California (1994), and Saguaro, Arizona (1994).

Today it is sometimes hard to savor the values of Yosemite and other parks that Frederick Law Olmsted perceived in 1865. But sublime scenery still has the potential to disrupt thought processes, liberating the mind from daily cares and fostering spiritual renewal. Meditation and recreation in spectacular natural environments remain good sources for personal health and vigor. Preservation of the unique landscapes and natural resources in parks has public support, especially among those who use them. Most park-goers do understand these values of nature, but they have to work a bit harder now to know national parks as they were meant to be experienced. It is not so easy to escape the city.

Clearly, the way people experience national parks is changing. The era of automobile tourists having open access will end with the present generation. Already, the Grand Canyon is planning to curtail automobile traffic on the south rim. A light rail system is being built to transport visitors from the gateway community of Tusayan to a new transit center at Mather Point. Alternative fuel buses, either electric or natural gas powered, will serve routes within the park. Trains and buses will be designed to suit visitors of all ages and abilities. Visitors with overnight lodging, camping, and recreational vehicle reservations will still be permitted to drive to designated parking areas for

their accommodations, but once inside the park, they will be required to use the transit system.

In 1996 the National Park Service held a transportation symposium in Fresno, California, to investigate various modes of transportation in and around Yosemite. Like the Grand Canyon, the most controversial proposals for Yosemite recommend limiting the access of automobile tourists in the park by constructing large orientation and transfer facilities where tourists will be required to park their cars. They will have to use public transportation to move in and around the park. The disastrous flood of 1997 helped clear the way for implementation of these plans to reduce traffic congestion, along with the removal of nonessential buildings, the restoration of some large natural areas, and the relocation of tourist and employee accommodations away from environmentally sensitive or dangerous areas.

At the opening of this essay, I proposed an imaginary journey to Yosemite, and the beautiful photographs in the volume will certainly fuel such flights of fantasy. At the dawn of the new millennium, we must in conscience suggest alternatives to "doing the parks" in the traditional sense of automobile tourists, the purpose of preserving these extraordinary tracts of the national landscape remains as Frederick Law Olmsted stated in 1865, to reinvigorate the visitor: "There is little else that has this quality so purely." Nothing compares with experiencing the scenery, wildlife, and historic sites of America's spectacular national parks firsthand.

Acadia

MOUNT DESERT ISLAND ON THE COAST OF MAINE IS THE glorious result of 500 million years of geologic activity: rivers laying down bedrock, volcanic ash turning into islands, magma reshaping rock. Ice-Age glaciers—migrating ice sheets up to two miles high—violently resculpted the mountains, then melted into the sea, creating islands and the continental United States' only fjord, Somes Sound. Today Acadia National Park covers much of Mount Desert Island, which French explorer Samuel Champlain named for its "bare mountains," perhaps the only feature of the foggy coast visible when his ship ran aground on its shoals in 1604. Europeans began settling here in 1759. In the 1800s, artists Thomas Cole and Frederick Church came to enjoy the island's fresh simplicity, and tourists followed. Mount Desert Island became a summer getaway for affluent industrialists—Rockefeller, Vanderbilt, Carnegie, Ford, Morgan, and Astor built opulent estates here. One visitor, George B. Dorr, seeing the threat from development and portable sawmills, began to acquire land on Mount Desert for the public's perpetual use, offering 6,000 acres to the federal government in 1913. John D. Rockefeller Jr. contributed 11,000 acres, where he had built woodland carriage paths closed to automobiles (cars are still banned on these roads today). In 1919 Wilson signed the act establishing the donated land as Lafayette National Park, the first national park east of the Mississippi. In 1929 its name was changed to Acadia—from "Arcadia," as explorer Giovanni Verrazano had designated the New World's East Coast in the 1520s.

Today the park covers 40,000 acres; its sixty-two square miles are spread over a dozen islands. The natural features of Acadia are a powerful blend of ocean and mountains. The forested slopes of Isle au Haut plunge right into the ocean. The sea surrounds and insinuates itself into the landscape, creating tidal pools that host an abundance of marine animals. The water life of Acadia ranges from algae and periwinkles to whales, and lobster buoys dot the ocean. Naturalist-led sea cruises visit the habitats of porpoises, seals, eagles, and seabirds, or the Islesford Historical Museum on Little Cranberry Island. Five lighthouses sweep the area—thick fog regularly obscures the seascape.

Astride the tidal zone, forested mountains slant to a spectacular view from the highest peak on the eastern seaboard, Cadillac Mountain, named after an erstwhile French resident who later founded Detroit. The woodland foliage is much different from Acadia's

original spruce and firs because of a tremendous fire in 1947 that burned 10,000 acres of the park. Sun-loving deciduous trees populate the forests, which can be explored on Rockefeller's carriage roads—circling Jordan Pond, bicycling around Eagle Lake, skirting brooks where beavers build their dams, climbing Sargent and Penobscot Mountains to reach breathtaking views of Frenchman Bay and Somes Sound. Acadia has more than 120 miles of trails, from idle surf walks to the challenging Precipice Trail.

Acadia is open year-round; the main visitor center operates from May 1 to November 1. The Park Loop Road provides a twenty-seven-mile scenic excursion by car, but it is jammed with traffic by midday in July and August, so get up early, or travel by foot or bicycle on the carriage roads or trails. Getting to Isle au Haut takes planning, worth it for the camper or hiker. Schoodic Peninsula on the mainland offers sensational views, less congested than Mount Desert's. June is best for fishing and birdwatching, though shore birds flock to the outer islands in July and August—Acadia's 275 species of birds include the endangered peregrine falcon. Leaf watchers throng in late September. Snow and ice close some roads from December to April to all but cross-country skiers.

—Susan Burke

View from the top of Cadillac Mountain to Frenchman Bay, dotted by small islands

Evening light illuminates
fissures in the granite rock
atop Cadillac Mountain

Jordan Pond is famous not only for its bucolic hiking trails but for the popover muffins served at its eponymous restaurant. On the north horizon are the Bubble Rocks.

Early morning at Otter Cove

A quiet cove along Frenchman Bay

Southwest Harbor lies at the
southwest entrance to Somes Sound,
the only fjord in the Lower 48 states.

Shenandoah

"SHENANDOAH" IS AN INDIAN WORD MEANING "DAUGHTER of the Stars." On some clear nights in Shenandoah National Park, the stars above the mountain ridges indeed seem as close as a loving parent. The park, named for the legendary river flowing below its western flank, begins in the Blue Ridge Mountains of northwest Virginia. Its single vehicular thoroughfare, the Skyline Drive, stretches 105 miles south to the Blue Ridge Parkway. Shenandoah National Park is a demonstration of "going back to nature," reversing the effects of farming that began in the eighteenth century when settlers from the north came to the fertile river valley. When land became scarce, people cleared the rugged forested mountains for farming, and by the twentieth century, the mountain soil was wearing out, trees were thin, game was scarce. The federal government took an interest in preserving this segment of the Appalachians, seventy miles from Washington, D.C., and Congress authorized the establishment of Shenandoah National Park in 1926. The Commonwealth of Virginia purchased 280 square miles of land from the remaining mountain residents; some sold voluntarily, other were relocated under vigorous resistance.

Remnants of farmhouses are still evident in the park's backcountry. But under the protection of the Park Service, Shenandoah has reverted to a mature forest, 95 percent covered with deciduous and evergreen trees. Two-fifths of the park is now designated wilderness. Whitetail deer are abundant and visible. Black bear inhabit the backcountry (and sometimes come near the Drive). Bobcats, skunks, possums, squirrels, chipmunks, as well as several species of salamander and the poisonous timber rattlesnake and copperhead, make their home in the park. About 200 species of birds have been spotted here—ruffed grouse, barred owls, woodpeckers, thrushes and thrashers, thirty-five species of warblers, scarlet cardinals and tanagers, Carolina wrens and goldfinches, indigo buntings, hawks, vultures, ravens, and wild turkeys.

But it is the quiet beauty of the landscape that attracts visitors in every season. In early spring, hepatica, red maple, and serviceberry show their colors, and soon the ground is covered in wildflowers, especially trillium and bloodroot. In April and May, as the trees begin greening, magenta redbud, wild white dogwood, and pink azaleas fill the woods with color, followed by fragrant black locust and pink and white mountain laurel. Deep, peaceful green is summer's dominant color, while wildflowers with names like Monkshood, Indian Paint Brush, and Pale Touch-Me-Not brighten up the forest floor. The first chilly nights of September launch autumn's colors. From the top, the ridges move into blazing vermillion, burnished bronze, deep ochre, peaking, ebbing, and peaking again as the various species alter their hues in turn. Finally, when winter descends, the deciduous trees create a starkly beautiful counterpoint for the evergreens, and the views of the valleys are cleared of the mists of summer. Now the Skyline Drive's many overlooks present the most far-reaching vistas—the Shenandoah River's seven bends, Signal Knob across the valley, the 360-degree view from Bearfence Mountain.

There are several entrances to the Skyline Drive between Front Royal and Rockfish Gap. The park is also accessible by the Appalachian Trail—a 101-mile section runs through the park—and 400 more miles of trails of various lengths provide access to much of the park, including its many waterfalls. Big Meadows, the only large cleared area at the center of the park, has a lodge and restaurant for visitors. Accommodations also include another lodge at Skyland, cottages, campgrounds, and six trail huts; backcountry camping is also possible. The park is open year-round, except when roads are closed by ice and snow. The speed limit on Skyline Drive is thirty-five miles an hour, but in autumn leaf season, traffic goes at a crawl.

—Susan Burke

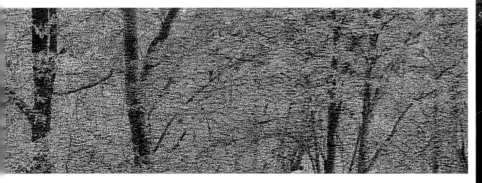

The autumn foliage along the Blue Ridge Parkway seen through a prismatic filter that simulates the pointillism of such painters as Georges Seurat.

Cascade in Dark Hollow, Shenandoah

Sunset view from Bearface
Mountain in April

Great Smoky Mountains

THROUGH THE HIGH, HAZY AIR OF THE GREAT SMOKY Mountains, the ghosts of the Cherokees who once ruled this rugged mountain land move silently between the trees. The deciduous forests, however, are evidence of a much older history, and the mountains themselves are some of the oldest on the face of the earth, formed 200 million years ago. The trees that established themselves here during the last Ice Age, having moved south to avoid the devastating effects of the glaciers, are notable for their diversity. Because Great Smoky Mountains National Park has more types of trees than do all the forests of Europe combined, it has been designated an International Biosphere Reserve. The Cherokee Indians were the first to live on this land within recorded human history, establishing a territory that extended from Virginia to Georgia and Alabama. But when white settlers moved in during the nineteenth century, the Cherokee were dispossessed of their land; now only a small number of their descendants are left on a reservation southeast of the park. By the 1920s, logging and pulpwood companies owned 85 percent of the 808 square miles that are within the present-day park, and they harvested freely. The rest belonged to thousands of small farmers and homeowners. Congress established Great Smoky Mountains National Park in 1926 to protect the high mountains, low valleys, rugged terrain, and extensive variety of flora.

The Smokies have more than 1,500 different types of flowering plants, providing visitors, especially hikers, with a visual cornucopia. In the spring, the wildflowers spread out through the woods and fields in a blaze of color. In June and July, the blooming rhododendron bushes are tall, up to twenty feet high, and form solid banks of pink and white and magenta. A hike to Gregory's Bald in late June will be rewarded with a profusion of wild azaleas along the edge of the meadow. In autumn, the exceptional variety of deciduous trees all turn color in their own way, searing the land in brilliant earth hues, especially in the valleys. Cool evergreens decorate the mountain heights, and above 6,000 feet the forests are similar to those of central Canada. The enormous botanical bounty of the Smokies is attributed to the rich soil and abundant rain, and the smoky blue haze, a finely tuned fog that sometimes becomes profuse, adds a dewy patina.

The park has many streams and waterfalls—destination points for hikers. Another backcountry attraction is finding the occasional log cabin or barn that originally belonged to an early settler, and now has been restored to recreate a view of the past for the present-day sightseer. The views throughout the Smokies are often spell-binding, especially on the road to Clingman's Dome, at 6,642 feet the highest peak in this range of mountains. An observation tower atop Clingman's Dome offers panoramic views.

Great Smoky Mountains National Park can be tasted by automobile—Newfound Gap Road provides a scenic route along the Smokies' crest—but to savor the park requires getting out and walking. The park has 850 miles of walking, hiking, and horse trails, with every range of difficulty. So all hikes don't have to be a same-day round-trip excursion, there are ten developed campsites, some requiring reservations to be assured of a place—and backcountry camping is allowed with a permit. A seventy-mile stretch of the Appalachian Trail that follows the border between Tennessee and North Carolina tempts hikers with a six-to-eight-day journey, with shelters about a day apart from each other.

—Susan Burke

Top: Rare snowfall on autumn foliage

Bottom left: Cades Cove preserves vestiges of pioneer life: more than 650 people lived in the broad, high valley by 1850.

Bottom right: White-flowering dogwood and budding leaves portend spring in the forests of the Great Smokies

Above: Little River

Dawn illuminates successive ridges of the >>> mountains visible from Foothills Parkway at the north edge of the park.

Biscayne

THE WORDS "BLUE" AND "GREEN" DON'T BEGIN TO describe it. "Turquoise," "azure," and "emerald" more truly suggest its extraordinary qualities. But perhaps any adjective limits the quintessential purity of the simple elements that compose this beautiful aquatic landscape— the water, sky, and shore of Biscayne National Park. A remarkable feature of this park southeast of Florida's peninsula is that 95 percent of its 283 square miles lie under the waters of Biscayne Bay. The park's official map shows green lines of land slicing through blue background on three sides, encompassing a smattering of keys, the largest ones dissecting the marinescape, and the boundary anchored on the west along a thin strip of shoreline. Biscayne Bay was explored early: Ponce de Leon plied its waters in 1513 searching for the Fountain of Youth. For the next couple of centuries, pirates preyed on unwary trading ships in the bay; Black Caesar apparently was based in the current park area. Later fishermen harvested the abundant fish and bay sponges, farmers planted crops, tourists and smugglers visited frequently. Shipwrecks littered the offshore bottoms. Eventually Miami became a super-developed world sprawling a few miles from the park's northern edge. By the mid-twentieth century developers were casting their eye on the bay's desirable keys, planning resorts and subdivisions, and a refinery was proposed on its shore. Bay lovers rallied to save its pristine nature, and in 1968 Biscayne Bay was declared a national monument. This area was subsequently enlarged and became a National Park in 1980.

What was saved? A subtropical world that combines a rare mixture of land and sea life, often echoing the Everglades ecology twenty-one miles westward. From the tiny sea horse to the enormous sea cow (nickname of the peaceful, galumphing manatee), marine animals abound in the crystal waters. The fishes of the reef are as brilliantly colorful as a summer garden, and as exotic as their names—queen angelfish, parrotfish, neon gobie, grunt. Sea turtles, moray eels, starfish, and octopuses cruise beneath the bay's surface. The ten-foot herbivorous manatee, whose numbers are flagging, grazes on underwater grasses. Shoreward, tropical birds like the white ibis and brown pelican are at home, and many migratory birds pass through. Growing in the islands' forests are rare mahogany, coppery-barked gumbo-limbo, satin-leaf, devil's-potato— a wealth of tropical plants.

The extraordinary inhabitants of bay and shore are protected in subtle ways by their environment. Mangrove swamps and forests put down an intricate tangle of roots that provide impenetrable nurseries for many varieties of fish. The mangroves also provide a buffer between the mainland and the bay, holding back eroded soil and pollutants from the water and protecting the land from hurricane-force winds. Biscayne protects the only living coral reefs in the United States. Colonies of tiny polyps thrive in this warm and shallow water producing limestone and building the reefs that shelter a huge variety of fish and marine life.

Biscayne's waters are the natural destination for the visitor. The bay is so clear and shallow that many exquisite fish are visible to snorkelers. Scuba divers can go deeper to explore the underground cities of the coral reefs. Glass-bottom boat tours allow fish-gazing with dry feet. Fishermen (with the required Florida saltwater license) go out for grouper, snapper, and sea trout, and for more challenging varieties such as marlin and sailfish. Convoy Point, the mainland base of the park, has wonderful views of Biscayne Bay from its boardwalk and the park visitor center. A park concessioner at Convoy Point offers tours and excursions to the barrier islands, which are accessible only by boat. Three keys—Elliott, Adams, and Boca Chita—provide public areas for camping and hiking, and free docking.

—Susan Burke

RIGHT: **A thicket of woody roots elevates a mangrove above the waters of Biscayne Bay.**

BELOW: **Underwater, the delights include swimming with sea turtles and surveying the intricate forms and vivid coloration of a live coral reef.**

OPPOSITE: **Schooling fish**

Everglades

FROM THE AIR, FLORIDA'S EVERGLADES RESEMBLE A verdant, pock-marked moon. But the view on the ground reveals the infinite complexity of this water-based landscape, as endangered as it is rare. The first crusade to keep the Everglades alive began with a murder on the heels of a massacre at the turn of the century. Because thousands of beautiful birds living here were killed in great numbers for their decorative plumes, the National Committee of Audubon Societies hired a warden to patrol the Everglades; when he was murdered in 1905, it inspired a movement to protect this remarkable ecosystem. Citizen lobbying and fund-raising, and state financing to

purchase private lands, finally convinced Congress to establish Everglades National Park, dedicated in 1947. But almost immediately, economic interests built huge dikes and canals to divert water for agriculture and real estate. The life force of the Everglades was threatened, seriously reducing the bird and aquatic populations.

These pressures continue to this day. Agricultural runoff disturbs vegetation patterns, and water-control structures near the park alternately shut off or flood the Everglades. The National Park Service, in partnership with Congress and the state of Florida, is working to restore the fresh water that is so essential to the life of the "river of grass." This river fifty miles wide and six inches deep, which supports sawgrass as tall as ten feet, flows from north to south through the Everglades into Florida Bay. The Everglades are larger than Delaware, 2,343 square miles, none more than eight feet above sea level. The river and its environs are populated by a remarkable variety of plants, animals, and especially birds. Among fourteen endangered species of animal living here are the wood stork, short-tailed hawk, and peregrine falcon, the huge and gentle vegetarian manatee and the green sea turtle, the Everglades mink and the Florida panther. The salt water supports the rare crocodile; alligators roam the freshwater streams. The rivers, bays, and ponds teem with crustaceans and fish, including large-mouth bass, snapper, redfish, and trout.

More than 400 species of birds inhabit the Glades:

roseate spoonbills, yellow- and black-crowned night herons, kites and egrets, pelicans and ibises. The Everglades are an important stop for migratory visitors on their way from North or South America. Hardwood hammocks support mahogany trees, strangler figs, gumbo-limbo with its copper-colored peeling bark, royal palm, and orchids. Hundreds of miles of mangrove rivers wind through the southern end, and closer to the ocean are mangrove thickets, an important shelter for land and sea life. Cape Sable, at the southernmost point of the United States, features white beaches and desert vegetation.

Boaters travel on marked canoe trails through the bays and rivers; the inland and coastal waterways lead to more remote areas. Hiking the many boardwalks and trails is an excellent way to see the park, which is accessible to automobiles only on the main park road. Flamingo, not far from the eastern entrance, is the base for sunset tours to bird-roosting grounds in Florida Bay and wilderness trips to Whitewater Bay, the Florida Bay keys, the Gulf, and Cape Sable's beaches. Everglades City in the north provides boat tours to Ten Thousand Islands and the mangrove swamps. Summer in the Everglades is warm and wet, full of mosquitoes. In the much drier winter, it is easier to see the animals as they gather around the limited water supplies. Look out for poisonous snakes, and avoid swimming, which could mean an encounter with an alligator, shark, or barracuda.

—Susan Burke

ABOVE: **Sandhill cranes find abundant food in the river of grass that is the dominant feature of the Everglades.**

BOTTOM RIGHT: **This great blue heron displays the white plumage of its immature phase.**

Paurotis palms and freshwater marl

OPPOSITE: **Florida Bay seen at sunset from near the town of Flamingo**

Mammoth Cave

ESTABLISHED IN 1941, MAMMOTH CAVE NATIONAL PARK features the longest known cave system in the world. This water-formed labyrinth, located beneath about eighty square miles of rugged hill country in southwest Kentucky, is a puzzle that defies completion. More than 330 miles of passages have been surveyed and mapped to date, and new ones continue to be discovered.

A combination of circumstances created this underworld wonderland millions of years ago; it continues to grow today primarily as the result of plentiful rainfall. The roof of the cave is a cap of shale and sandstone, which lies above subsurface limestone. Rainwater erodes this limestone into passages by seeping through the surface in places called sinkholes. Also dissolving the limestone into passages are horizontally flowing underground streams, which carved the cave's five known levels. The oldest level is at the top; the youngest at the bottom. As the Green River, which runs east to west through the park, sliced more deeply into the valley, so did the cave streams. Today, cave streams are carving new passages at depths of up to 450 feet below the surface.

Because Mammoth's cave system was created predominantly by horizontally moving water, it offers relatively few travertine formations, which are the handiwork of vertically moving water carrying dissolved limestone. One breath-taking exception is Frozen Niagara. Unlike the names of other cave formations, which as Mark Twain noted can be "overdescriptive," this massive seventy-five-foot-tall and fifty-foot-wide orange-white flowstone is no misnomer. Flowstones occur when water pours over ledges; stalactites grow as water drips from the ceiling; and stalagmites rise as water droplets accumulate on the cave floor.

The cave's temperature is always about 54°F. Its residents include troglobites, or "cave dwellers," creatures who never leave the darkness and therefore have dispensed with such unnecessary attributes as eyes and skin pigmentation. Twelve species, including the Mammoth cave shrimp, are found only here. Others like the blonde cricket are "cave guests" or trogloxenes because they must make nightly food forays to the surface to survive. This group includes the little brown bat, which can consume some 600 mosquitoes in a single hour. Two of the twelve kinds of bats that frequent the cave are endangered. Overall, more than 200 different species of wildlife are known to use the cave. Mammoth is both a World Heritage Site and an International Biosphere Reserve, in part because of the cave's unique and vulnerable ecosystem.

Twelve miles inside the cave are open to the public for guided tours. These range from a rugged five-mile, six-hour, belly-crawling, spelunking challenge to a seventy-five-minute, thirty-six-step trip to see shimmering stalactites and stalagmites. The Historic Tour, a two-hour, two-mile excursion, features folklore as well as geology: it visits the Rotunda, where seventy slaves mined saltpeter to make gunpowder for the War of 1812, and such marvels as Mammoth Dome, a 192-foot-high shaft created by a dripping sinkhole. Five types of tours are offered throughout the year; during the summer months, visitors have twelve different tour choices.

Above ground more than sixty miles of trails traverse Mammoth Cave National Park, including ones to River Styx Spring and Echo River Spring where water from the cave flows into the Green River. From May through October, a one-hour, scenic boat excursion on the Green River is offered. Canoe and horse rentals are another way to explore the park. Mostly second-growth woodlands of sycamore, hickory, oak, and hemlock dominate the landscape, and nearly 900 species of flowering plants infuse it with color. The diversity of wildlife reflects that of an eastern hardwood forest while the Green River sustains an unusual array of bird and aquatic life, including several fish and freshwater mussel species that live here and nowhere else.

—Leslie Croyder

Banded stalagtites in limestone

Hot Springs

THE SMALLEST OF THE NATIONAL PARKS, AT JUST OVER eight-and-a-half square miles, Hot Springs prefers to emphasize that it is the "oldest area in the park system" because President Andrew Jackson designated the area as a special U.S. reservation in 1832. Located about an hour's drive from Little Rock, Arkansas, its fame arises from the mineral-rich, thermal waters that flow from Hot Springs Mountain. Long before Hot Springs National Park was established in 1921, this natural resource had been tapped to supply several city blocks of bathhouses along Central Avenue, now restored to simulate the heyday of the spa in the early years of this century. Tourists have sought out these waters since 1561, when Hernando de Soto and his party are reputed to have bathed here.

At the heart of Hot Springs National Park today is a small city with many charms, surrounded by low-lying mountains in a horseshoe formation. Known as the Zig Zag Mountains, they comprise the eastern edge of the state's Ouachita Range. Above them rises Hot Springs Mountain, where on its lower western side, the "discharge zone," forty-seven hot streams flow, most of which have been covered by the park to prevent contamination of the "healing" waters. The park also protects the "recharge zone," where rain and snow that soak into the ground replenish the springs over time.

Prized because it is naturally sterile, the water bubbles from the park's springs at about 143° F. Some 4,000 years elapse in the natural process of converting snow or rain into hot mineral-rich water. As the water seeps through cracks and travels deeper beneath the earth's surface, the increasingly warmer rock heats it, filtering out the water's impurities. At the same time, the water dissolves minerals in the rock. Eventually it meets the faults and joints in the sandstone leading up to the lower western side of Hot Springs Mountain where it flows to the surface. Because its rise to the earth's surface occurs relatively quickly—in about two years—the water has little time to cool off. Approximately 850,000 gallons of water flow from these springs each day, coursing through a complex system of pipes into the park's reservoir, which supplies Hot Springs' commercial baths and the "jug fountains," where visitors can sample the drinking water.

The park's visitor headquarters, located on Central Avenue, is a twenty-three-room museum featuring gleaming plumbing and luxurious baths. This "temple of health and beauty" replicates the furniture and equipment used to treat and pamper patrons between 1915 and 1920, a regime that in its full form involved three weeks of daily baths and massage. At nearby Buckstaff Bathhouse, today's visitors can enjoy the soothing effects of bathing in hot springs waters, and hotel bathhouses are also open to the public.

In all seasons but winter, rangers lead walking tours to the open hot springs. Visitors can also access trails, most of which begin at Central Avenue, for independent explorations. By following the Hot Water Cascade trail, visitors will spot tufa—a milky-colored, porous rock formed by mineral deposits being created at the rate of one-eighth inch a year by the cascade's splashing waters. These waters sustain only two life forms: blue-green algae and the ostracod, a crustacean the size of a sand grain. Visitors who want to touch the hot mineral waters in a natural setting should select the trail to Open Springs where two springs flow into a collecting pool.

The park offers a single campground, which accommodates both tents and trailers, about three miles from downtown at Gulpha Gorge. Park trails here lead hikers through forests of oak, hickory, and short-leaf pine. Early spring features an understory of blooming redbud and dogwood. And during autumn, the park presents an arresting array of fall colors, which can be viewed from scenic mountain drives.

—Leslie Croyder

LEFT: **Oak forest in the Zig Zag Mountains.**

RIGHT: **View to Central Avenue's Bathhouse Row from the surrounding forest.**

Voyageurs

THE LOVELINESS OF VOYAGEURS NATIONAL PARK LIES in its watery beauty. One-third of the park's area is water, most of it in four lakes. Voyageurs stretches for fifty-five miles along the U.S.-Canada border, encompassing some thirty lakes and more than 900 islands. Established in 1975, it is Minnesota's only national park and one of America's premier boating parks.

This lake country is a gift from glaciers, huge and heavy sheets of ice that overrode the area at least four different times during the last one million years. As the glaciers retreated northward, lakes formed in their wake. Kettle lakes, common throughout this park, were made by giant ice blocks that broke apart from glaciers and were left behind, buried in debris to thaw slowly over many centuries, creating water-filled depressions.

The great northern coniferous forest is an important part of the park's patchwork landscape of lakes, bogs, streams, and marshland. Both untouched virgin stands and second-growth habitat comprise these forested areas. Black spruce, tamarack, cedar, ash, and willows grow in the lowlands. The rockier and drier upland areas support red, white, and jack pine, as well as white spruce, balsam, and aspen. And beneath all of this terra firma are rock types, mostly granite, that hint of Voyageurs' origins 2.7 billion years ago.

Thriving in the park's lowland areas are clumps of paper birch, easily recognized for their white, papery bark. This tree best symbolizes the spirit of Voyageurs, named in honor of the French Canadians who paddled birch-bark canoes for fur-trading companies in the late eighteenth and early nineteenth centuries. Renowned for their stamina as well as their songs, these voyageurs established a canoe route between Canada's northwest and Montreal that was cited as a border in the treaty that ended the American Revolution.

The 340-square-mile park consists of four large lakes—Rainy, Kabetogama, Namakan, and Sand Point—a strip of mainland shore, and the Kabetogama Peninsula, in addition to myriad smaller lakes, islands, and waterways. It is open year-round to visitors, although freezing temperatures limit access between late fall and early spring. Winter visitors rely on snowmobiles, snowshoes, cross-country skis, and ski-planes. Summer visitors travel by foot or floatplane, usually renting or towing in motorboats, houseboats, or canoes. Many hire experienced guides to help them navigate park waters.

Most visitors find lodging and facilities to access Voyageurs' landscape at one of four resort communities situated just outside the park: Kabetogama Lake, Rainy Lake, Crane Lake, and Ash River. For those with limited time, Kabetogama Lake is an ideal choice. From this base, hiking, boating, and canoeing are all options, with or without guides. Some visitors select a quick ride across the lake by boat, followed by a two-mile hike to Locator Lake where they pick up a cached canoe they had rented earlier. Another appealing alternative is the all-day cruise to Kettle Falls, a historic waterways hub used by Native Americans, voyageurs, and other frontiersmen. This cruise stops for lunch at the clapboard-style Kettle Falls Hotel, which was originally built in 1910 to cater to lumberjacks and continues to host overnight guests who reserve well in advance.

Whether it's snowmobiling in the winter or waterskiing in the summer, the park presents an extraordinary array of visitor activities. It also offers respite to those who prefer quiet camping, either on the water or in the woods. Walleye, northern pike, and smallmouth bass await anglers. Wildlife watchers, too, will be rewarded. Voyageurs' year-around residents range from the shy black bear and beautiful red fox to the industrious beaver, playful river otter, and majestic bald eagle.

—Leslie Croyder

Left: **Algae bloom colors the waters of Kabetogama Lake.**

Right: **Cranberry Creek flows from Locator Lake and snakes through the pristine woodlands of Minnesota's only national park.**

Namakan Lake is one of the largest
lakes in this watery wilderness.

Reindeer lichen

Isle Royale

A WILD AND RUGGED ARCHIPELAGO, ISLE ROYALE National Park is situated in Lake Superior's northwest corner, accessible only by boat or floatplane. Its isolated setting has made it something of an anomaly among national parks: it inspires three-and-and-half-day stays, whereas the average visit to a national park is only four hours. Its visitors linger, but there aren't many of them: backpackers account for about half of the 18,000 people who journey to Isle Royale each year, but Yellowstone sees more people in a single day. This isolated realm in Michigan's Keweenaw County was established as a national park in 1940, and in 1981, it was designated an International Biosphere Reserve.

Ponds, streams, rivers, and surrounding Lake Superior waters comprise 80 percent of Isle Royale's nearly 900 square miles. Around the forty-five-mile-long island are more than 400 smaller islands. Seen from above, Greenstone Ridge, which runs the length of Isle Royale, looks like the park's backbone. Isle Royale rose above what would become Lake Superior when the last glacier that sculpted this landscape, known as the Wisconsin, retreated 10,000 years ago.

The origins of Isle Royale, however, go back much further, to a time when a great rift in the earth's crust spewed molten lava, which covered thousands of square miles. The land along the rift zone subsequently sank to form the Superior Basin. The park's bedrock, 1.1 billion years old, records this cataclysmic event as a mixture of basalt lava flows, sandstone, and conglomerate that contains no fossils. As these rock layers tilted and eroded, they created the ridge-and-trough pattern that is visible today. The high ridges are composed of hard basalt, while the valleys are areas where the weathered sandstone eroded.

Isle Royale's two ports, Rock Harbor and Windigo, welcome visitors from mid-May through mid-October and offer a wealth of options for adventuresome travelers. Boat reservations, which should be made several months in advance, leave from three locations: Grand Portage, Minnesota; Houghton, Michigan; and Copper Harbor, Michigan. The shortest trip to the island is two hours, one way from Grand Portage to Windigo; traveling to Rock Harbor takes two to three times longer. Most visitors bring their own gear for "leave no trace" camping at backcountry sites ideally suited to savoring Isle Royale's pristine wilderness. Those with seaworthy boats may explore the islands at their leisure. Noncampers who reserve well in advance can stay at Rock Harbor Lodge, the untamed island's only lodgings, with eighty units.

With more than 165 miles of foot trails, hiking is a popular way to explore the island. Balsam fir, white spruce, and white birch grow along the coastal regions; sugar maple and yellow birch thrive on inland ridges, and in the swamplands, black spruce presides. Among the park's most famous residents are immigrant wolf and moose populations, which have been the subject of predator-prey studies by biologists for nearly fifty years.

Once a French territory, Isle Royale retains its name from this chapter in its past. Naturalists lead guided tours—by boat, canoe, and foot and recount the island's history, including its days of copper mining and commercial fishing, as well as the natural history of the park. Boat cruises take visitors to the outer islands. Fishing is good year-round, but particularly during the fall and spring. Scuba divers are welcome to prowl the major wrecks around Isle Royale, including the *America*, a 183-foot lake steamer that sank in 1928.

—Leslie Croyder

The rising sun illuminates the watery paradise of Isle Royale

OPPOSITE: **A rocky inlet on Tookers Island near the northeast end of Isle Royale National Park**

<<<

The shores of Lake Superior create a tranquil hideaway.

A view of the island wilderness preserve that is Isle Royale National Park.

Theodore Roosevelt

IN HONORING THE MEMORY OF THE COUNTRY'S TWENTY-sixth president, Theodore Roosevelt National Park also pays tribute to the "badlands," a fantastic terrain of rock formations, famous for their strange shapes and stripes that were created by wind and water. Established in 1978, the park brings together three sites on the western edge of North Dakota, all of which share the Little Missouri River. In this climate of extremes, where earthly forces create unworldly formations, Roosevelt tried his hand at cattle ranching between 1884 and 1896. As president, he established five national parks and founded the U.S. Forest Service. Roosevelt considered his decade in the badlands one of the events that shaped his life, reflecting, "I never would have been President if it had not been for my experiences in North Dakota."

Buttes, tablelands, and valleys distinguish the landscape of these badlands. Its origins go back 65 million years to the epoch when the newly arisen Rocky Mountains sent streams carrying sediments to this area that later would be carved by the Little Missouri River and its tributaries. Today this deposition and erosion of sediments continues.

The bewildering beauty of the badlands provides ample evidence of erosion's mighty hand. Slump blocks lay toppled on valley floors, having gradually slid intact from steep canyon walls. The stripes of these oversized jigsaw pieces provide clues that link them to the bluffs from where they came. These parent bluffs have eroded too, moving farther back from their original position. Caprocks, also called pedestal rocks, look like giant mushrooms. Their tough tops protect the sediments beneath them while the softer sediments around them crumble away. Among the park's other works in progress are polished rocks with peculiar shapes. Fierce, sand-carrying winds created these signature pieces of the badlands. The brick-colored bluffs of the badlands are not volcanic, although this rock material is known locally as scoria. It formed when a layer of black lignite ignited, turning the surrounding clay and sand into a kind of natural brick.

With rainfall scarce, the park's vegetation is rigidly stratified. In sunny, southern spots where water evaporates quickly, little grows but grasses. The relatively moist northern slopes support junipers and in the valley, near the river, tall cottonwoods thrive. Wildflowers burst into bloom from early spring to late fall. Bison, elk, and pronghorn, native to this area, are some of the park's largest inhabitants. The badlands are also home to prairie dogs, rattlesnakes, and many songbird varieties, including the meadowlark, a particular favorite of the former president. Two non-native species reside within the park, as they did during Roosevelt's days: a herd of longhorn cattle and bands of wild horses.

The park's three units, which together preserve 110 square miles, are separated by seventy miles. Although the park is open year-round, summer is an ideal time to visit; the days are long and a full program of activities is offered.

During winter some park roads close due to inclement weather. In all seasons the park's population of visitors is surprisingly sparse. Exploring the North and South Unit calls for combining car travel with foot trails; renting horses is another option at the South Unit. For those with a day or less to spend, the South Unit features a scenic, thirty-six-mile loop road, as well as the greatest collection of petrified wood in the park. The third section of the park, located between the North and South Unit, was the site of Roosevelt's Elkhorn Ranch, where only the foundation markers of his second residence remain. This undeveloped site is accessible to visitors, depending on road conditions.

—Leslie Croyder

Cannonball concretions are among the odd features created by erosion and wind-blown sand in the badlands.

The Little Missouri River carved many of the formations of the badlands.

Badlands

TO UNDERSTAND BADLANDS NATIONAL PARK, ONE MUST travel back in time to see how the land it protects was named. Native Americans and European explorers could spare little praise for this stern and sometimes scary place. The Lakota knew the area as *"mako sica."* French trappers called it *"les mauvaises terres à traverser."* Roughly translated, each means "bad lands." Today approximately one million people visit this 381-square-mile park—located some seventy miles from Grand Rapids, South Dakota—to experience it for themselves. Established in 1978, it encompasses three sites: easiest to navigate is the North Unit; to the south, not far from where the White River flows, are the Stronghold and Palmer Creek Units, which lie in the Pine Ridge Reservation and are managed under a cooperative agreement between the Oglala Lakota and the National Park Service.

Going deeper into history helps explain the park's geological treasures and unnerving terrain. Approximately 75 million years ago, it was part of a large area that was under water. Another ten million or so years later, with the pushing and shoving of the continental plates, the Rocky Mountains erupted, causing this shallow sea to retreat and drain away. During the millions of years that followed, the climate was warm and wet, and a subtropical forest flourished. Gradually, as the weather grew cooler and drier, the forest became a savannah, which in turn became the grasslands of today. Typically tiered and sometimes smooth, the park's spectacular rock formations were eroded by water over eons. Most awesome of these is the Wall, a desolate band of cliffs, pinnacles, buttresses, and gorges. One-half to three miles wide, this colossal-sized landmark is the park's scenery belt.

Frozen in time within the park's badlands are fossils. Once the sea's bottom, the grayish-black sedimentary rock called the Pierre offers a look at such ancient invertebrates as Baculites, an extinct cephalopod with a squidlike body and a long cylindrical shell tightly coiled at one end. The colorful red bands of buttes contain fossils from the Oligocene era, which lasted from 23 to 35 million years ago. These fossilized soils, so prevalent in the park, provide pictures of extinct mammals, large and small. These include the sheeplike Oreodonts; Paleolagus, an ancestral rabbit; Metamynodon, a huge and hefty rhinoceros; and Hoplophoneus, among the first animals to be called a saber-tooth cat.

The park today is North America's largest remaining mixed-grass prairie. Capably coping with too much trampling and not enough rain, as well as frequent fires and ferocious winds, some fifty-six species of short and long grass anchor the park's diverse wildlife community. Bison and bighorn sheep, once badlands denizens, have been successfully reintroduced to the park. Black-footed ferrets are the park's newest residents. The dramatic return of this endangered species to its former habitat is the result of captive-breeding efforts.

The park's enormous expanse requires visitors to explore it by car as well as on foot. Both off-trail hiking and backpacking are permitted. The North Unit, which offers a year-round information center and overnight accommodations in a lodge and campground, features a scenic, eighty-nine-mile loop road with plenty of pullouts, nature walks, and self-guided trails. With one hundred square miles, Sage Creek Wilderness is ideally suited for spotting wildlife.

Visitors ready to weather rougher conditions will find the South Unit an adventure to remember. Sheep Table Mountain offers perhaps the park's most spectacular view of classic badlands scenery. And those prepared to put wear and tear on their cars, willing to open and close a good many gates, and able to use a topographical map will eventually find sacred grounds on Stronghold Table. Here, the final Ghost Dance occurred in 1890, days before more than 150 Lakota were massacred at Wounded Knee, twenty-five miles to the south.

—Leslie Croyder

LEFT: Badlands from Sheep Table Mountain

RIGHT: The red-banded buttes of the badlands are a treasure trove of Oligocene-era fossils.

OPPOSITE: The Wall, a band of rock formations that is three miles wide in some places, is a landmark of the prairie.

Wind Cave

ALL THAT'S BEAUTIFUL ABOUT WIND CAVE NATIONAL Park does not lie beneath its surface. Situated in South Dakota's southwest corner, it was established in 1903 as the country's seventh national park to safeguard a cave of seemingly endless proportions. Less than a decade later, however, the park's sunlit ecosystem also became the focus of protection. Plant and animal species common to the eastern and western United States coexist here, in an uncommon world where the mixed-grass prairie of the western Great Plains meets the ponderosa pine forests of the Black Hills.

The spectacular cave that inspired the park's creation was named for the strong winds that rush in and out of it, equalizing air pressure between the passages inside and the atmosphere outside. It was the sound of these whistling winds that led brothers Jesse and Tom Bingham to the cave's only natural opening in 1881. Local entrepreneurs subsequently explored and exploited Wind Cave, selling pieces of its exquisite mineral formations and offering tours for fees based on the number of candles required to complete them. Commercial ventures such as a stagecoach trip from nearby Hot Springs billed Wind Cave as "the Great Freak of Nature."

After more than a century of exploration, Wind Cave today is one of the longest caves in the world, known to have more than seventy-eight miles of passages. But according to barometric wind studies, only about 5 percent of the total cave has been discovered to date. The red clay and sandstone sediments found in its older sections were deposited by an ancient sea approximately 320 million years ago. The cave's newer passages began forming about 60 million years ago when the nearby Black Hills were lifted by the same forces that created the Rocky Mountains. As a result, large cracks split the limestone layers beneath the present-day park. During the millions of years that followed, water seeped through these cracks, slowly dissolving the limestone into a labyrinth of passages.

Rare and fragile mineral formations adorn the walls of Wind Cave, where the temperature holds steady at 53° F. A calcite formation called boxwood that looks like irregular honeycombs is present in great numbers. This unusual collection is considered one of the world's foremost. The cave, however, creates few of such well-known mineral formations as stalactites and stalagmites because water is scarce here. Throughout the year, guided tours showcase the cave's splendors. The summer features a fuller schedule, including a two-hour, candlelight trip that harkens back to the 1890s and a rough trek, twice the length, that involves real exploration of the cave.

Approximately 75 percent grasslands, the park preserves a piece of the great plains that remains much as it appeared to westward-bound, eighteenth-century pioneers. It also features a transitional prairie-and-pine-forest environment, where species indigenous to the eastern and western United States live alongside one another. Among the park's most celebrated inhabitants are its bison, elk, and pronghorn. Wiped out in the 1880s largely from uncontrolled hunting, these animals have

been returned to their former range. The park's bison, which number about 350, are descended from fourteen animals donated by the Bronx Zoo in 1913. Visitors today have unparalleled opportunities to see these shaggy behemoths because the park they roam is less than forty-four square miles.

Scenic roads, where bicyclists are welcome, wind through the park's prairies, forests, and hills. There are thirty miles of hiking trails, as well as two self-guided walks. One offers a panoramic view; the other takes visitors through an area in the park where forest and prairie meet. Picnicking in a ponderosa pine woodland is another possibility. Visitors may stay overnight in the park campground, which is open from April through October, or to enjoy backcountry camping.

—Leslie Croyder

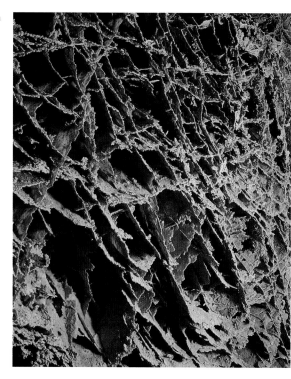

Top Left: **Boxwood, a calcite formation, lines many of the passages within Wind Cave.**

Top Right: **Prairie dogs build dams and tunnels to protect their homes from wind and water.**

Bottom: **Bison have been reintroduced to their former rangelands, a transitional prairie-and-pine-forest environment.**

Opposite: **A double rainbow arching over prairie grasslands suggests the view that eighteenth-century pioneers may have witnessed during their journey westward.**

Big Bend

AS THE RIO GRANDE FLOWS SOUTH ALONG THE BORDER of Texas and Mexico, the river swings abruptly north before turning back again to continue its journey into the Gulf of Mexico. Within the horseshoe-shaped piece of the Chihuahuan Desert, outlined by the Rio Grande, lies Big Bend National Park. This remote park of more than 1,200 square miles features unforgettable panoramas of the surrounding badlands. Punctuating this landscape are volcanic mountains, steep, narrow canyons, and lush floodplains where junglelike vegetation grows. The weather is harsh and unpredictable here, but the wildlife diverse.

The Rio Grande flows along the park's southern side for 118 miles, cutting through three major canyons—Santa Elena, Mariscal, and Boquillas. Mountains dominate Big Bend's skyline. Comprised mostly of shale and limestone deposits made by ancient seas, they were uplifted about 75 million years ago, causing the center of the park to sink. At the park's heart rise the Chisos Mountains, the southernmost range in the continental United States, which were created by volcanic activity some 35 million years ago.

Some 10,000 years ago, piñon-juniper forests extended to the desert floor, but their range gradually retreated as the climate warmed slowly. Elevations range from 1,800 feet at the eastern end of Boquillas Canyon to 7,825 feet atop Emory Peak in the Chisos Mountains, and the vegetation varies accordingly. Desert shrub becomes sotol grasslands then piñon pine, juniper, and oak woodland. Altogether more than 1,000 plant species have been identified in Big Bend, including sixty types of cactus that brighten the desert landscape with sequential waves of colorful bloom.

Over 400 kinds of birds have been spotted in Big Bend, more than in any other U.S. national park. These include the endangered peregrine falcon, whose nesting areas the park protects, as well as the gray-and-yellow Colima warbler who migrates from the Mexican state of that name to raise its young here and nowhere else in the country. The park's most amazing native was one that lived in the age of the dinosaurs. The Quetzalcoatlus, a Texas pterosaur with a thirty-five-foot wing span, was the world's largest creature known to fly.

Exploring Big Bend calls for a reliable car and sturdy walking shoes. About thirty miles of the park's hiking trails are moderate-to-easy. The Chisos Basin is a favorite spot among hikers. Horseback riding and bicycling are other options, although rentals are not available inside the park. For an especially exciting perspective of Big Bend, visitors can take float trips on the Rio Grande. Once among the roughest white water in the country, its rapids have been calmed somewhat by dams that provide water and power to desert communities, but excursions, which range from one day to two weeks, still provide thrills and a closer look at this Wild and Scenic River. The Chisos Lodge offers cottages as well as rooms, and the park's campgrounds and backpacking camping sites are rarely full except during major holidays.

At Big Bend there's no shortage of places to see or stories to hear. The drive from Panther Junction to Persimmon Gap, which follows the trail used by raiding Comanche parties, encourages visitors to take short side trips to examine an exhibit of dinosaur fossils, marvel at the giant yucca's seventy-pound stalks of showy blossoms, and explore Glenn Springs, a pioneer town abandoned after it was raided in 1916. A different route offers visitors the chance to picnic at Dugout Wells, near a spring where wildlife gather, before traveling further east to the Mexican border town of Boquillas for sightseeing on horseback. Visitors only need to decide which aspect of the park interests them most.

—Leslie Croyder

RIGHT: **View of the Sierra Quemada from the south rim of Chisos Mountains.**

BELOW: **The Rio Grande flows through the cut-rock walls of Santa Elena Canyon.**

OPPOSITE: **The spiky forms of a century plant echo the craggy peaks of the Chisos Mountains, a relatively young range at the heart of Big Bend National Park.**

Guadalupe Mountains

SUDDEN THUNDERSTORMS AND DIAMONDBACK rattlesnakes may not be celebrated in Guadalupe Mountains National Park, but they are part of its rugged character. Here, less than an hour's drive from Carlsbad Caverns, the southernmost, highest part of the fifty-mile-long Guadalupe Mountains rises above the seemingly barren plains of the Chihuahuan Desert. About half of the 135-square-mile park is designated wilderness. Part desert, part canyon woodland, and part highland forest, the beauty of this west Texas park lies in the land's diversity.

Outside the state, the park is something of a secret among tourists. It was established in 1979 after the Park Service acquired several ranchlands in the area, among them land in McKittrick Canyon, donated by petroleum geologist Wallace Pratt in 1959. Currently the park is acquiring another 10,000 acres, including colorful dunes of quartzose and gypsum, deposited by a tropical ocean that covered portions of Texas and New Mexico more than 250 million years ago.

Geologists worldwide marvel at the Guadalupe Mountains, which share the same underwater origins as New Mexico's Carlsbad Caverns, as well as the Apache and Glass Mountains located to the south. All are part of an ancient marine fossil reef known as the Capitán. (For information about the formation of this 400-mile-long limestone reef, see Carlsbad Caverns National Park.) This extraordinary reef grew above everything else in Texas, creating Guadalupe Peak. At 8,749 feet, its spectacular views of the surrounding desert are unlike those of 15,000 years ago when conifer forests covered the region. Today this forest of ponderosa pine, southwestern white pine, Douglas fir, and aspen survives only in the park's mountaintops and some of its higher-elevation canyons.

This highland wilderness is home to a variety of large mammals, most notably mountain lions, black bears, and elk. Hunted to extinction in the early 1900s, the park's elk, a herd of about sixty animals, are descendants of a group brought from Wyoming and South Dakota in the 1920s. Among the birds to inhabit the highlands are wild turkeys, vultures, golden eagles, and the endangered peregrine falcon. Lizards and snakes are abundant in the desert; here, too, coyotes and mule deer have been spotted. The most likely places to find wildlife, however, are the park's shady canyons and desert springs.

McKittrick Canyon, sometimes described as the most beautiful spot in Texas, shelters the park's only year-round stream. Growing along its banks are grey oak, velvet ash, and bigtooth maple, as well as the rare and picturesque Texas madrone, easily distinguished by its smooth, reddish bark and evergreen leaves. This five-mile-long canyon brings together a diverse mix of life from the highlands above as well as the desert below. Here mountain lions frequent the same pools as mule deer. Other four-footed inhabitants include jackrabbits, coyotes, porcupines, gray foxes, and elk. Open for day use only, this oasis features a shady spot for picnics and several trails of varying lengths, including one that offers glimpses of the park's geological past.

More than eighty miles of trails, open to both hikers and horseback riders, traverse the park, ranging from easy walks to arduous climbs. The park also offers two campgrounds and ten backcountry camping sites. Dog Canyon features scenic trails into the park's remote, northern highlands. Further south, hikers have many options. These include a short stroll to what remains of the 1858 Pinery Station of the Butterfield Overland Mail; a two-mile loop trail to two desert springs; and strenuous excursions to Guadalupe Peak and the Bowl, a lush forest located 2,500 feet above the desert. El Capitán, the southernmost bluff of the Guadalupes, rises 8,085 feet above the desert floor. This enduring symbol of the frontier looms large on the landscape.

—Leslie Croyder

El Capitán, the southernmost peak of the Guadalupe Mountains, looms 8,085 feet above the desert floor.

OPPOSITE: Rippled gypsum sand dunes of the Chihuahuan Desert meet the Guadalupe Mountains.

Carlsbad Caverns

SEVENTY-FIVE STORIES BELOW THE EARTH'S SURFACE IS a cave system of such staggering dimensions that Will Rogers described it as the "Grand Canyon with a roof on it." Colossal-sized cavities, carved by sulfuric acid, show-case cave decorations from the delicate to the gigantic. Inside the Big Room, large enough to encompass fourteen football fields, is a sixty-two-foot-high stalagmite along with two other forty-two-foot-high cave formations. The cave's fame also derives from the spectacular nightly flight of its Mexican free-tailed bats, which summer in one its upper chambers.

Established in 1930, Carlsbad Caverns National Park is located in New Mexico's southeastern corner, not far from the border of the Lone Star State. Above ground it is seventy-three square miles of unassuming, arid habitat. Its lower elevations belong to the Chihuahuan Desert, a grasslands community that supports a variety of succulents. Its upper elevations, to the west, are also grasslands although this landscape of the Guadalupe Mountains includes more tree and shrub types, particularly pine, oak, and juniper. Spring and fall are ideal for spotting desert flowers—from either the gravel loop road, less than ten miles long, or the half-mile, interpretive trail that describes the native flora and how it was used by Indians.

The park's appearance today offers few clues, for the layman, to indicate that this region was covered by saltwater 250 million years ago. The marine plants and animals that lived in the Permian Sea left a legacy that grew into a horseshoe-shaped reef more than 400 miles long after their remains settled at the sea's bottom. When the sea dried up and disappeared, the Capitán reef stood hundreds of feet high. But it, too, vanished from sight, buried slowly by tons of sediments thousands of feet deep. This pressure compacted the animal shells and plant remains into limestone and caused the Capitán to

crack. Hydrogen sulfide gas, left by the Permian Sea, seeped inside the Capitán. Mixing with water, it turned to sulfuric acid, carving the limestone into huge cavities. Not until the reef was uplifted some 20 to 40 million years ago, when the Guadalupe Mountains were created, did the sulfuric acid drain out of the reef.

The cave's dazzling decorations began to take shape when air flowed inside the reef for the first time a million years ago. Seeping through decaying plants and animals, surface water picked up carbon dioxide. This acidic water percolated through the reef, carrying with it infinitesimal limestone particles. It deposited these particles on the ceiling, walls, and floors of air-filled openings. The result was an array of glistening formations in all shapes and sizes, from nests of cave pearls and a forest of soda-straw stalactites to silky flowstone draperies worthy of a queen's chambers. Perhaps the most beautiful of these are aragonite trees, once thought to be alive. Sparkling like intricately cut diamonds, these formations can take root just about anywhere, sprouting spiny branches that subdivide again and again.

Today the sound of dripping water inside Carlsbad Caverns is rare, as this desert region receives less than nineteen inches of precipitation annually. Of its twenty miles of passageways discovered so far, three are open to visitors. The main cavern features several tours, including a one-hour, one-mile walk around the Big Room. Another option—for those who don't mind crawling—is a two-hour, flashlight tour of Slaughter Canyon Cave, open during winter weekends and summer months. Between May and October, visitors gather outside Carlsbad's main cavern at sunset to witness the amazing exodus of some 5,000 Mexican free-tailed bats per minute. Airborne on eleven-inch wings, each one weighs about half an ounce. Most are mothers who return at sunrise to communally nurse their young.

—Leslie Croyder

Pictographs in the Painted Grotto provide evidence of human habitation in ancient times.

OPPOSITE: **Totem pole formation dominates the Big Room at Carlsbad Caverns.**

Petrified Forest

LOCATED WITHIN ARIZONA'S PAINTED DESERT, PETRIFIED Forest National Park preserves a unique piece of the Colorado Plateau. Once part of a vast floodplain crossed by many streams, this arid land of badlands hills, flat-topped mesas, and buttes contains one of the world's largest concentrations of brilliantly colored petrified wood. Protecting these remarkable deposits is an ongoing challenge for the park, which has developed numerous strategies, including stiff fines, to reduce theft. Each year, however, more than 900,000 people visit the park and, according to studies, leave with some twelve tons of wood.

The temptation to take is not new. Not long after military survey parties passed through the region in 1851, stuffing their saddlebags with petrified wood, fossil logs were being hauled off by the wagonload to become tabletops, mantels, and other ornaments. Soon gem collectors were dynamiting the logs in search of amethyst and quartz. To prevent further destruction, the area was designated as the country's second national monument in 1906. Nearly sixty years later, it became a national park with expanded boundaries. Today more than half of this 143-square-mile park is designated wilderness.

Nearly all of the park's petrified wood comes from tall conifers called Araucarioxylon that grew in distant highlands more than 200 million years ago. Uprooted by either floods or mudflows, these trees, which resembled modern Norfolk pines, were washed into logjams and then buried by silt and ash. This blanket of deposits diminished the flow of oxygen, causing the wood to decay more slowly than it would have otherwise. Mineral-carrying water later seeped into the wood, and slowly, bit by bit, multicolored quartz replaced its organic tissue.

Sparkling like oversized jewels, giant fossilized logs lay scattered throughout the park. Many are the size of cordwood. The largest concentrations of petrified wood can be found in the park's southern section. Here short walks from pullouts lead to sensational sights: logs, up to 120 feet long, crisscrossed in logjams; shimmering cross-sections of fossil trees; and "Old Faithful," the largest fossil log in the park with nearly a ten-foot diameter.

As it has for eons, erosion continues to slowly undress the park, revealing up to 300 feet of fossil-bearing remains in some places. So far scientists have identified more than 150 different plant and animal species, which date from the late Triassic Period about 225 million years ago. The park's museum vividly portrays life back then—when the park was filled with streams, ferns, and cycads, and the toothless, two-ton Placerias was among the least dangerous dinosaurs. Only much later did the region sink, become submerged by freshwater sediments, and then uplifted. No permanent streams run through the park today; this high desert grassland receives less than nine inches of precipitation annually.

Within the park are many sites that reflect prehistoric American Indian settlements, including Puerco Ruins, an Ancestral Puebloan village. Several dozen people lived in its seventy-six rooms surrounding a plaza, farming collectively—and successfully enough to survive the long drought that devastated many communities in the Southwest—but it too was abandoned in the early 1400s. Petroglyphs, carved images made by pecking away at the dark mineral stain covering the boulders, are found throughout the park. The meaning of this ancient art, which includes animals, kachinas, tracks, and geometric designs, remains a mystery. But some of the carvings, including an elaborate series within the Cave of Life, are illuminated by the sun at precise moments in the seasonal cycle and so have gradually been recognized as an ancient stone calendar.

From eroded escarpments banded in blues and purples to wide-open vistas dominated by intense reds and softer shades of pink, the views from the park's scenic road are strangely beautiful. Open all year, weather permitting, this twenty-eight-mile road connects the southern petrified forests with the Painted Desert Wilderness Area to the north where visitors can camp and hike.

—Leslie Croyder

ABOVE: A herd of pronghorns forage near the buttes of the Painted Desert.

RIGHT: The massive size of the petrified logs is evident in this panoramic view.

OPPOSITE: A logjam of petrified trees, an extinct species of conifers that grew 200 million years ago.

Saguaro

SAGUARO WAS ESTABLISHED IN 1994 AS THE SOUTHWEST'S newest national park, enlarging an existing two-section national monument that takes in parts of two desert mountain ranges, bracketing the city of Tucson. Like Sequoia/Kings Canyon and Joshua Tree, Saguaro was created primarily to protect one particular plant, in this case, the giant saguaro cactus, the largest cactus north of Mexico.

Although saguaros are native only to the wettest of North America's four deserts, the Sonoran Desert of Arizona and northern Mexico, these commanding cacti, growing as tall as fifty feet, with as many as a dozen upraised arms, have come to symbolize the entire arid Southwest. They are, as Frederick Turner writes in *Of Chiles, Cacti, and Fighting Cocks*, his meditations on the American Southwest published in 1990, "the generic cactus that stands for... all those lands 'out there' in the West."

Saguaros are engineering marvels, beautifully evolved to deal with the desert's extremes of heat and drought. Like most cacti, they store water in their own tissues in order to survive in a land where rain is rarer than not. With a network of fine roots stretching out in a skirtlike pattern into the soil around its trunk, a large saguaro can take up as much as 200 gallons of water after a single rainstorm. Weighing up to eight tons when tanked up, a saguaro grows lighter and thinner as it uses its supplies. A strong but flexible skeleton of ribs arranged in a column supports a saguaro's great weight and, along with the plant's accordion-pleated skin, allows it to expand and contract with its fluctuating water supplies.

As the largest "trees" in their desert, saguaros are more than a symbol for their arid ecosystem: they house or feed literally hundreds of desert creatures. Holes in their trunks provide cool, shaded homes for dozens of hole-nesters from Gila woodpeckers to purple martins; hawks build platform nests in the crotches of saguaro arms. Long-nosed bats, white-winged doves, bees, moths, and other creatures dine on the nectar and pollen from their night-opening blossoms; the sugary, figlike fruits feed javelinas, coyotes, foxes, rodents, harvester ants, wasps, birds, and humans. Fallen saguaros shelter desert creatures from cactus mice to western diamondback rattlesnakes; their decaying flesh nourishes a whole other community of lives.

Although Saguaro National Park was established to protect the "forests" of these giant cacti, the park offers far more. With two rainy seasons per year, one in summer and one in winter, the Sonoran Desert is the most verdant of North America's deserts, home to more species of cacti, shrubs, and wildflowers than any other desert. Because of its paradoxically lush vegetation, more kinds of animals—from velvet ants to desert tortoises, from roadrunners to javelina— live here as well.

Saguaro West, the section of the park west of Tucson in the Tucson Mountains, includes the densest saguaro forest known. These groves of giant cactus are easily seen from the main road, as well as from the nine-mile-long Bajada Loop Drive beginning at the visitor center. Several trails afford close-up views of these remarkable cacti and their rugged home, including the wheelchair-accessible Desert Discovery Nature Trail and the more strenuous King Canyon Trail, which climbs a wash, or a normally dry streambed, into the rocky Tucson Mountains, topping out at 4,600 feet with a panoramic view of the Tucson Basin and surrounding mountains.

Less-visited and larger Saguaro East, an hour's drive across Tucson in the Rincon Mountains, also protects dense saguaro groves. Cactus Forest Drive, an eight-mile scenic loop road beginning at the visitor center, winds through this venerable forest. But the real enchantment of this section of Saguaro is accessible only by foot or on horseback along the 128-mile network of trails, which take visitors from hot desert to cool montane forests, akin to a journey from southern Arizona to southern Canada. Sitting next to a spring high in the Rincons, amidst towering ponderosa pines and Douglas fir trees, the searing sunlight and saguaro cacti of the desert seem worlds away.

—Susan J. Tweit

RIGHT: **Spiral petroglyph in the Sonoran Desert**

BELOW: **The giant saguaro cactus is slow-growing, but many reach fifty feet in height in the wettest of the southwestern deserts.**

OPPOSITE: **A storm at sunset illuminates the sturdy trunks of blooming saguaro cactus and the crinkly diagonals of ocotillo.**

Grand Canyon

ON A TRIP INTO THE MILE-DEEP GORGE IN 1903, President Theodore Roosevelt declared the Grand Canyon "the most impressive piece of scenery I have ever looked at." In 1908 he set aside the main part of the canyon as a national monument; it became a national park in 1919. In the 1960s, the federal government proposed flooding more than half the length of the canyon behind two dams. The dams were defeated, and in 1975 the park was expanded to 1,875 square miles, protecting the entire length of the Inner Canyon.

Ranging from four to thirteen miles wide, as deep as 6,000 feet, and 277 miles long, this is truly a "grand canyon," North America's most awesome chasm. The layers of rock that form this spectacular gorge tell a story of the past 2 billion years of the continent's evolution, recording the crash of continental plates, the advance and retreat of great seas, the rise and erosion of whole mountain ranges, the formation of immense fields of sand dunes, and the explosions of volcanoes near and far.

Although the rocks that form it are old, the canyon itself is relatively new, carved by the Colorado River during the past 5.5 million years. Geologists theorize that the river now slices right through a bulge in the Colorado Plateau, whereas it once ran around it, draining into a lake basin in northeastern Arizona. Then, some 5 million years ago, the San Andreas Fault system opened up the Gulf of California, giving a new, thousands-of-feet-lower outlet to a small stream that was eroding headward into the bulge. This stream broke through into the historic drainage of the Colorado River, capturing the much larger stream and its erosive power to carve the Grand Canyon. Summer flash floods and spring snowmelt continue to enlarge the canyon.

From piñon pine-juniper woodlands on the canyon's South Rim to Mojave Desert in the canyon bottom to spruce-fir forests on the North Rim, the Grand Canyon spans a dizzying diversity of ecosystems. A trip from the Inner Gorge, at an elevation of 2,400 feet, where summer temperatures may reach a sizzling 115° F and snow is rare even in winter, to the North Rim at more than 8,000 feet, where summers are cool and snow closes the roads from mid-October until May, is like traveling from Baja California to British Columbia. The ever-widening gap of the canyon itself has also created new species by isolating populations of animals and plants, including a pair of formerly similar tasseled-ear squirrel species: the gray-and-white Abert squirrel of the South Rim and the black-and-white Kaibab squirrel of the North Rim.

Humans have inhabited the Grand Canyon for at least 4,000 years, beginning with the Desert Culture, creators of the split-twig animal figures found in caves below the rim. Havasupai and Hualapi Indians still live along the southern side of the canyon. Tourists have flocked to Grand Canyon since the Bright Angel Trail was built in the 1890s. Today Grand Canyon National Park attracts some five million visitors a year, most to the more-easily-accessible South Rim. Traffic congestion has become such a problem, in fact, that mass transit will eventually replace private vehicles on the South Rim.

"At first glance the spectacle seems too strange to be real," wrote Joseph Wood Krutch about the Grand Canyon in 1957. Although it is possible to see the canyon by simply driving up to a viewpoint on the South Rim, walking a trail or riding the river immerses the visitor in the canyon's awesome reality. On the congested South Rim, the Rim Trail affords a more solitary experience of the canyon in early morning or around sunset. Trails plunging down from the Rim are strenuous but reveal magnificent views as they drop a vertical mile to the Colorado River. The much-less-visited North Rim, 220 miles away by paved highway and a thousand feet higher than the South Rim, reveals an entirely different Grand Canyon, with dense forests, wildflower-splashed meadows, and spectacular vistas. Raft trips ranging from three days to three weeks take visitors down the river itself into what explorer John Wesley Powell called the "Great Unknown," the heart of the Grand Canyon, a world of turbulent water and cathedral-like canyon walls.

—Susan J. Tweit

Above: **Piñon-pine sapling rooted on sandstone above the Colorado River at Toroweap.**

Foldout: **Golden light floods the chasm of the Grand Canyon, seen from Mather Point on the South Rim.**

Mount Hayden dominates this view from
Point Imperial on the North Rim.

A dusting of snow transforms
the view from Maricopa Point.

Havasu Falls on the Havasupai Indian Reservation

Tourists at the Desert View Overlook

Zion

ISAAC BEHUNIN, A MORMON SETTLER, WAS SO AWED BY Zion Canyon's sheer sandstone walls, topped by magnificent tan and white rock buttes, that he declared, "These great mountains are natural temples of God." Utah's oldest national park was designated a national monument in 1909 by President Taft and enlarged to 229 square miles and made a national park in 1919.

Soaring 2,000 feet from valley floor to plateau top, the walls of Zion Canyon are among the highest sheer cliffs in North America. The normally shallow and clear Virgin River doesn't seem powerful enough to have carved this canyon, but its impressive drop—it tumbles 80 feet per mile in places, ten times that of the Colorado River in the Grand Canyon, as it falls from a 9,000-foot elevation at the top of the Markagunt Plateau to 4,000 feet in the canyon bottom—combined with its flash flood potential—the river swelled fiftyfold in just fifteen minutes during a storm in 1954—give the Virgin River awesome grinding power.

Water on a smaller scale creates some of the most enchanting features of this xeric landscape: weeping walls and hanging gardens. Water trickling down through pores and fractures in the two thousand-plus-foot-thick layer of Navajo sandstone hits impervious shales and siltstones lying beneath and runs along the top of the shales, eventually emerging from cliff faces and canyon walls, nourishing lush "hanging gardens" of water-loving plants including orchids, columbines, and ferns.

The most popular part of Zion National Park is Zion Canyon, visited by 2.5 million people a year. Most enter the park by the Mount Carmel Highway, which plunges from the top of the Markagunt Plateau down into Zion Canyon via two tunnels—the second of which is over a mile long—and six switchbacks. Zion Canyon Scenic Drive, which branches off the Mount Carmel Highway near the South Entrance, gives views of many of the park's most famous landforms, including the Great White Throne, Angels Landing, and Weeping Rock. It ends at the Temple of Sinawava, where visitors can continue on foot up the Narrows, the upper canyon of the Virgin River.

Because of vehicle congestion and narrow spaces, large vehicles are restricted in parts of Zion Canyon and on the Mount Carmel Highway. Beginning in the year 2000, Zion Canyon will be accessible only by shuttle bus from March to October.

Trails are the best way to experience Zion Canyon. An easy and non-strenuous half-mile trail leads to Weeping Rock, a lush garden created by groundwater "weeping" from a Navajo sandstone wall. The Angel's Landing Trail, which ascends the West Rim of the canyon, yields spectacular views but is not for the fainthearted: it climbs 1,500 feet in two-plus miles, zigzagging up the canyon walls in a hair-raising route including "Walter's Wiggles," twenty-one switchbacks named after the first park superintendent. The park's most famous trail may be the Narrows, a twelve-mile one-way hike/wade up the North Fork of the Virgin, where the 2,000 foot-high canyon walls constrict in places to just thirty feet wide. Because of the danger of flash flooding, hikers in the Narrows must obtain a permit, but visitors can walk the one-mile paved Riverside Trail to its mouth to see why the Paiute Indians named the canyon *Ioogoon*, or "arrow quiver."

Zion's wildest and least visited area is Kolob Canyons, accessible via a short paved road off Interstate 15. Here, trails lead into narrow canyons with sculptured landforms including Kolob Arch, the world's largest natural rock opening, with a span of 310 feet. Autumn is the best time to visit these quiet canyons as the cottonwood, boxelder, ash, and bigtooth maples lining the small streams blaze gold and scarlet against rust-red rock walls.

RIGHT: **Virgin River landscape**

LEFT: **Towers of the Virgin are snow-capped in this winter view.**

BELOW: **To witness sunrise at Observation Point, photographer Liz Hymans hiked more than two hours through the pre-dawn darkness to an elevation of 6,508 feet, 2,100 feet above the valley floor.**

OPPOSITE: **The force of the Virgin River, which carved Zion Canyon, is magnified by its precipitous drop.**

Bryce Canyon

BRYCE CANYON IS NAMED FOR MORMON SETTLERS Ebenezer and Mary Bryce, who homesteaded in the area between 1875 and 1880. After moving away, Ebenezer Bryce reportedly said of the pastel-colored galleries of sculptured rocks that now attract 1.5 million visitors a year: "It's a hell of a place to lose a cow." Thanks to lobbying by supporters like J.W. Humphrey, then Supervisor of the surrounding Sevier National Forest, who once offered a skeptic ten dollars if he wasn't impressed by the view, Bryce Canyon National Monument was established in 1923; five years later, it was enlarged to its current size and designated a national park.

At fifty-six square miles, eighteen miles long and only five miles wide at its widest, Bryce Canyon is Utah's smallest national park. Geologically, it is not really a canyon, but a series of amphitheaters or natural bowls carved into the edge of the 9,000-foot-high Paunsaugunt Plateau, one of a string of high plateaus (Zion National Park occupies another) that rise above the slickrock desert of southwestern Utah. Unlike the hard sandstones that form Zion's massive cliffs and domes, however, the upper layers of the Paunsaugunt Plateau are fine, easily eroded mud- and siltstones. Streams and rivers deposited these sediments a thousand feet thick in a series of inland lakes 63 to 40 million years ago. Iron tints some layers soft rusty orange, manganese colors others blue-gray or lavender. Some ten million years ago, the whole area stretched apart, causing the rock layers to break along fault lines. Some sections, including the Paunsaugunt Plateau, "floated" upwards several thousand feet, while neighboring sections, like the Paria Valley east of Bryce Canyon, "sank." Streams eroding the raised edge of the plateau cut the soft, banded sediments into millions of finlike walls, spires, minarets, and hoodoos—pinnacles eroded into fantastic shapes such as Thor's Hammer, The Poodle, and Queen Victoria.

Ranging from an elevation just over 6,000 feet at the north end of the plateau, to more than 9,000 feet at its southern end, Bryce Canyon is a cool, moist refuge from the hot, arid desert below. Piñon pine-juniper woodlands and ponderosa pine forests cover its lower end; aspen, spruce, and fir, the highest elevations. Mountain grasslands provide a home for the Utah prairie dog, a colonial rodent included on the Endangered Species List and once exterminated from the area. Utah prairie dogs, were reintroduced to Bryce in the late 1970s, are gregarious animals whose extensive system of tunnels is crucial to turning over and fertilizing grassland soils. Recently, researchers have discovered that prairie dogs' whistling and barking calls comprise vocabularies sophisticated enough, for instance, to describe specific intruders: "Tall human approaching, behind you!"

The eighteen-mile park road, ending at Rainbow Point, follows the edge of the plateau for most of its length, offering spectacular views from spots including Fairyland Point, overlooking one of the most dense areas of hoodoos; Sunrise Point, perfect for watching the rising sun tint this extravagant landscape with soft colors; and the aptly named Inspiration Point. Fifty miles of trails,

both following the rim and dropping down below it into the crowds of hoodoos, offer close encounters with this wonderland of sculptured rocks. Below the rim, trails drop steeply in short distances, and because the overall elevation is high, return ascents may tax even the most physically fit hiker.

Paiute Indians, who summered in what is now Bryce Canyon National Park until they were driven out in the 1870s, believed the sculptured rocks were once birds, animals, and lizards that had the power to turn themselves into humans. According to the Paiutes, these early residents took to gambling and quarreling, so angering the god Shin-Owav that he turned them into stone. There they stand today, for all to see.

—Susan J. Tweit

BELOW: **The bowl-like form of Bryce Canyon is evident in this long view across the Paunsaugunt Plateau.**

RIGHT: **Queen's Court is one of the fanciful names inspired by the strange shapes of Bryce's pink rock formations.**

OPPOSITE LEFT: **The rising sun rakes the sculptured forms, brushed by new-fallen snow, at Sunrise Point.**

OPPOSITE RIGHT: **Thor's Hammer is a landmark on the Navajo Loop Trail below Sunset Point.**

Canyonlands

GEOLOGIST AND ONE-ARMED CIVIL WAR VETERAN Major John Wesley Powell put the area that is now Canyonlands National Park on the map—literally—in 1869, when he and his party successfully ran the Green and Colorado rivers, surveying the last blank space in the map of the United States. Near the confluence of the two rivers, the center of today's Canyonlands National Park, Powell wrote: "Wherever we look there is but a wilderness of rocks; deep gorges where the rivers are lost below cliffs and towers and pinnacles; and then thousands of strangely carved forms in every direction...." Nearly a century later, in 1964, the area was protected within Canyonlands National Park.

The 527 square miles of Utah's largest national park encompass what many consider the heart of the Colorado Plateau, a grand sweep of slickrock landscape whose massive rock layers have been sculpted by water and polished by the incessant winds. The region's two largest rivers, the Colorado and the Green, incise a giant Y through Canyonlands' rock layers, dividing the rugged landscape into three sections.

Wedged between the arms of the Y is the most accessible and heavily visited part of the park, Island in the Sky, a mile-high, triangular-shaped mesa reached by a paved road that ends at Grand View Point. Perched 2,200 feet above the Confluence, the hundred-mile-wide panorama visible from Grand View Point gives a sense of how immense and rugged this landscape really is. Visible far below are the two rivers, winding between rock walls; midway between the river canyons and the mesa edge is the pale thread of the White Rim four-wheel-drive road, traversing a lower mesa.

The Needles, named for a "forest" of striped sandstone pillars, lies east of Cataract Canyon, the main stem of the Y. A paved road leads into the area, but the best of it, a wonderland of sculptured rocks, fins, needles, arches, and slot canyons, lies beyond the pavement, accessible by foot, mountain bike, horse, and four-wheel drive. Along the rare permanent stream drainages are signs of earlier residents: the ruins of a cowboy line camp at Cave Spring; towers, rooms, and granaries built by the Ancestral Puebloan Indians (formerly called the Anasazi), who inhabited the area before A.D. 1300; and pictographs painted by the Fremont people even earlier.

The third and wildest section, The Maze, lies south of Green River, west of the stem of the Y, and can be reached only by a forty-six-mile unpaved road. Hiking trails lead down steep descents into tortuous slot canyons, which once hid Butch Cassidy and his gang. The convoluted passages preserve some of Canyonland's most spectacular pictographs, including the Harvest Panel and other huge godlike images left by the Fremont people at least 2,000 years ago.

The two rivers themselves form a world of their own, a thread of green and shade in the midst of dazzling sunlight and bare rock. From quiet floats along the Green to the exhilarating whitewater of the rapids in Cataract Canyon, described by Fred Dellenbaugh, a member of Powell's 1871 expedition, as like being "on the back of the Dragon," thousands of visitors experience Canyonlands by rafting or kayaking its rivers.

Although shaped by water, Canyonlands is desert-dry, receiving just seven to nine inches of precipitation a year, much of that in torrential summer thunderstorms. Despite the barren look of the landscape, however, life flourishes here, from the largest herd of desert bighorn sheep in the western United States to tiny freshwater shrimp that hatch as if by magic when natural potholes in the rock fill with rain or snowmelt. Canyonlands' most crucial lives, however, grow right underfoot in a bumpy layer called cryptobiotic crust. This community of microscopic lives protects and nourishes the droughty, nutrient-poor soils, forming a living sponge that prevents erosion, stores precious moisture, and fertilizes the soil. Because the filamentous threads that bind this living crust are fragile and take tens of years to repair, visitors are asked to tread carefully and stay on trails and roads.

Canyonlands is most popular in spring and fall, because winter brings snow and lows as extreme as -29˚F, and summer temperatures at the lowest elevations can sizzle as hot as 115˚F. No matter what the season, however, Canyonlands' "wilderness of rocks" works its magic.

—Susan J. Tweit

A wall of ancient painted figures and a cluster of striped sandstone pillars along Salt Creek, both typical of the Needles district of Canyonlands.

ABOVE: **Mesa Arch**

RIGHT: **Sandstone slabs above the Green River at Fort Bottom**

FAR RIGHT: **The White Rim and Soda Springs Basin viewed from Island in the Sky**

Capitol Reef

MORMON SETTLERS NAMED CAPITOL REEF FOR THE enormous conical sandstone domes that reminded them of the U.S. Capitol, sitting atop a redrock spine they called a reef. The reef itself is the spine of Waterpocket Fold, a hundred-mile-long wrinkle in the rock layers of the Colorado Plateau. Today's 378-square-mile Capitol Reef National Park, established as a small national monument in 1937 and enlarged sixfold and designated a park in 1971, is the only southwestern national park besides Grand Canyon to preserve an entire geologic feature, the long, narrow Waterpocket Fold.

This giant standing wave of rock is one of central Utah's most prominent landforms. Born some 65 million years ago when uplift of the Colorado Plateau raised one section of rocks and dropped the adjacent one, Waterpocket Fold is like a giant rock stairstep. Rather

than breaking at the fold, the great rock layers simply drooped over the displacement. Subsequent millennia of erosion have eaten through the fold to create a parallel sequence of ridges (formed by the erosion-resistant rocks) and valleys (the softer rocks).

Waterpocket Fold is named for rainwater-collecting potholes that pock its slickrock surfaces. Slight depressions in the rock collect water and are enlarged by the prying action of frost, eventually deepening enough to provide habitat for a unique community of aquatic lives that thrive in the brief weeks when the pothole fills with water and endure the long months when it is bone dry. As the water disappears, adult spadefoot toads, born and raised in the pothole, dig themselves into the mud at the bottom, encasing their bodies in a coat of water-conserving mucus. Gnat larvae dehydrate, losing up to 92

percent of their body water, yet can still swarm to life when water returns. Freshwater shrimp eggs lodge in cracks in the dried pothole bottom and can survive thus for decades.

Waterpocket Fold splits the landscape of central Utah like a wall, forming a formidable barrier to travel— the first paved road traversing it was not built until 1962. Of the two roads that cross it, only Highway 24, which follows the canyon of the Fremont River through the Fold's north end, is paved. Unpaved Burr Trail zigzags up and over the southern end.

The few canyons slicing the Fold, greened by permanent water, have harbored humans for at least 10,000 years, including the people archeologists call the Fremont because they inhabited the area watered by the Fremont River. They spread across the Colorado Plateau

in small settlements, cultivating flood-irrigated farms with unique varieties of maize, hunting, and gathering wild plants. The drought-stricken years of the 1200s pushed the Fremont out of Waterpocket Fold. Sometime later, the nomadic Utes and Paiutes arrived, moving from place to place with the seasons. In the late 1800s Mormon farmers settled along the Fremont River, planting fruit and nut orchards, which still yield delicious crops.

Highway 24 offers the easiest access to Capitol Reef, winding through the Fremont River canyon with its panels of mysterious Fremont petroglyphs and its views of Capitol Dome. A scenic drive branches off at the Visitor Center and runs south through Fruita and its lush oasis of orchards, then climbs up onto the spine of the Fold. Among the many hiking trails is an easy walk down Capitol Gorge, a narrow wash between sheer walls,

leading to the Pioneer Register, a rock signed by early travelers, and to several waterpockets.

The mostly unpaved Notom-Bullfrog Road, which parallels the east edge of the Fold, gives dramatic views of this great landform. Here, wildflowers flourish in season along the Bitter Creek Divide, including white cushions of phlox, Indian paintbrush, and the delicate, tuliplike blossoms of sego lilies, Utah's state flower. From the Burr Trail, the only road to cross over the Fold, the uptilted rock layers drop off steeply to the east, marching toward the distant peaks of the Henry Mountains. To the west, Burr Trail winds through the plateaus of the newly created Grand Staircase National Monument, just another piece of what the landscape writer and desert rat Edward Abbey called "a grand waste of largely naked sandstone, a slickrock wilderness."

—Susan J. Tweit

LEFT: **Storm above Waterpocket Fold, seen from Strike Valley Overlook**

BELOW: **The Castle and cottonwoods in autumn**

OPPOSITE TOP: **Moonrise over sandstone**

OPPOSITE BOTTOM: **Piñon pine below Hickman Bridge**

Arches

STEPPING OUT OF HIS PARK SERVICE HOUSE TRAILER before dawn on his first morning in Arches, new ranger Edward Abbey was captivated by the wild landscape of rust-colored sandstone studded with arches, monumental balancing rocks, finlike walls, and buttes. "This is the most beautiful place on earth," he wrote, beginning the journal that would eventually become *Desert Solitaire*. Others agreed. Designated a national monument in 1929, after officials of the Denver and Rio Grande Railroad lobbied director of the National Park Service Stephen T. Mather, Arches was enlarged in 1971, and made a national park.

Small enough to explore in a day, large enough to feel wild, 114-square-mile Arches is named for its unique concentration of natural rock openings—there are more here than anywhere else in the world. The park contains more than 2,000 natural arches, ranging in size from squeeze holes just three feet in diameter (the smallest opening that can be called an arch) to the longest one, Landscape Arch, measuring 306 feet from base to base.

The reason for the profusion of arches is a simple one: salt. Deep under the layer-cake arrangement of sedimentary rocks that makes up the Colorado Plateau lies a 3,000-foot layer of gypsum and other salts deposited by an ancient evaporating sea. Salt deforms under pressure. As sediments accumulated in ever-thicker, ever-heavier layers atop the layer of salt, the siltlike rock began to flow like warm silly putty, growing thinner where the overlying rock layers were thickest, doming up where the layers above were thinner. Arches sits on a dome, where the salt layer pushed up and cracked the overlying layers of sandstone in a regular pattern of joints. Over the eons, water, snowmelt, frost, and ice have seeped into the joints and flaked away at the rock, whittling it into thin, isolated fins, then carving big blocks out of the fins until holes cut right through, forming arches—thousands of them.

Arches' arches rise from a largely bare, slickrock "pavement" of yellowish or rust-red Navajo sandstone, a massive layer of fossilized dunes deposited in a Sahara-like desert millions of years ago. Stunted piñon pines and junipers dot the slickrock, rooting where soil collects in joints in the rock, and a riot of colorful wildflowers bloom from April to October, watered by snowmelt and summer thunderstorms. This seemingly barren landscape is home to the same desert-adapted animals as the rest of the Colorado Plateau, rattlesnakes to mountain lions, kangaroo rats to harvester ants.

Many of Arches' collection of arches and other rock sculptures are visible from the main road, which climbs from the Visitor Center up past Courthouse Towers and The Great Wall, and ends at Devil's Garden at the north end of the park. Here, the Devil's Garden Trail leads to Landscape, Double O, Pine Tree, and other arches clustering along the east side of the park's largest drainage, Salt Wash. The Windows section, accessible off a side road that leaves the main road not far from Balanced Rock (near the former site of Abbey's house trailer), contains another dense collection of arches, including North and South Windows and Double Arch, all

reached by short trails. Delicate Arch, perhaps the park's most famous arch, rises near the Cache Valley on the park's eastern edge.

Like most Colorado Plateau parks, Arches is hot in summer, with daytime temperatures routinely rising above 100° F, and bone-chillingly cold in winter. Spring and fall bring the most clement temperatures, but spring winds can whip up sandstorms, and fall may mean snow. Harsh, dry, forbidding—still, Arches is an intoxicating landscape. As Abbey wrote in *Desert Solitaire*, "In this glare of brilliant emptiness, in this arid intensity of pure heat,...all things recede...annihilating all thought and all that men have made to spasms of whirling dust far out on the golden desert."

—Susan J. Tweit

Top: **Delicate Arch at sunrise**

Right: **"Park Avenue"**

Opposite: **Turret Arch viewed through North Window at sunrise**

RIGHT: **Double-O Arch**

LEFT: **Balanced Rocks**

Mesa Verde

IN DECEMBER OF 1888, WHILE TRACKING COWS IN A snowstorm atop Mesa Verde, Richard Wetherill and Charlie Mason walked to the edge of a cliff and spotted Cliff Palace, the Southwest's largest cliff dwelling, in an alcove below. Excited, the two men lashed together a ladder of logs to descend the sheer cliff, and explored a city that had remained vacant for almost 600 years. Soon the Wetherill Family was guiding tourists to these ancient dwellings. Mesa Verde, the "Green Table" rising high above the Mancos River Valley in southwestern Colorado, became famous, attracting archaeologists, collectors, and pothunters alike.

In 1906 President Theodore Roosevelt signed legislation to establish Mesa Verde as the nation's sixth national park and the first one designated specifically to protect cultural resources. Named a World Heritage Site by the United Nations in 1978, Mesa Verde contains more than 4,000 known archaeological sites—and new ones are discovered each year.

Although a hunter-gatherer culture roamed this part of southwestern Colorado as early as 12,000 years ago, later arrivals, the Anasazi or Ancestral Puebloans, built the cliff dwellings that made Mesa Verde famous. Archeologists first named these people the Anasazi, a Navajo word which literally translates as "enemy ancestors." Modern-day Pueblo Indians, however, maintain that these "vanished" people were their ancestors, citing origin stories and cultural beliefs. Most archaeologists now call the Anasazi "Ancestral Puebloans."

The Ancestral Puebloans arrived at Mesa Verde around A.D. 550, drawn by the mesa's natural resources: the dense piñon pine—juniper woodlands atop the mesa, the seeps and springs along the massive sandstone cliffs, abundant wildlife including deer and turkeys, and the relatively flat, arable mesa top. At first, these people lived in pithouses, small, circular, earth-sheltered dwellings roofed with piñon and juniper branches plastered with mud. They farmed flood-irrigated fields, wove fine coiled baskets of yucca fiber and rabbitbrush, domesticated wild turkeys, and perfected pottery with distinctive black-on-white designs.

Some 200 years later, Ancestral Puebloan culture changed. They moved into larger villages on the mesa top and began to build with stone, eventually constructing many-roomed pueblos, multistory, apartmentlike dwellings built around a central courtyard surrounded by high stone walls. The masonry work rivals that of medieval Europe: each stone meticulously shaped into rectangular blocks, then carefully fitted in tight courses rising three and four stories high. Two large reservoirs and numerous smaller check dams built on the mesa top suggest intense farming and an increasing problem with drought.

Around A.D. 1200, Ancestral Puebloan life took another turn: the people moved out of their mesa-top pueblos and into hastily constructed cliff dwellings set in the sides of steep cliffs. Why they moved remains a mystery: perhaps to protect the cliffside seeps and springs, their drinking water sources; perhaps to save increasingly scarce firewood by taking advantage of passive solar heat.

After a century, the Ancestral Puebloans moved again, this time deserting Mesa Verde. The ancients seem to have simply walked away from the cliff dwellings, leaving behind their belongings, including pots full of corn, bows and arrows, jewelry, and in one case, a pair of crutches. Why did they leave? Most likely a combination of factors, including a region-long drought from 1276 to 1299, and overuse of local natural resources. Where did they go? To the upper Rio Grande, the Zuñi area of northwestern New Mexico, and the Hopi mesas in Arizona, places still inhabited by today's Pueblo Indians.

Mesa Verde National Park is reached by a paved road, which climbs atop the steep mesa and then winds down the gently sloping top to the two main areas of cliff dwellings and pueblo ruins: Chapin Mesa and Wetherill Mesa. Most visitors head for the cliff dwellings of Chapin Mesa, including 200-plus-room Cliff Palace and Balcony House, accessible only by a thirty-two-foot ladder and a narrow tunnel. On the way is Far View Site, with some of the finest examples of mesa-top pueblo construction. A drive out Wetherill Mesa, open only in summer, takes visitors away from the crowds to surprise views of cliff dwellings much like what Richard Wetherill and Charlie Mason glimpsed that snowy December day in 1888.

—Susan J. Tweit

Cliff Palace on Chapin Mesa

Great Basin

EXPLORER JOHN C. FRÉMONT NAMED THE ENORMOUS stretch of desert landscape between California's Sierra Nevada and Utah's Wasatch Range the "Great Basin" because water from its 210,000 square miles of flat-floored valleys goes nowhere, either evaporating from shallow playa lakes, or simply sinking into the ground. The Great Basin remains one of the wildest sweeps of western landscape, with mile after mile of narrow, high mountain ranges alternating "in lilting rhythm" with shrub-covered desert basins, writes Stephen Trimble in *The Sagebrush Ocean*, his natural history of the Great Basin, published in 1989.

Although only 120 square miles in size, Great Basin National Park, created in 1986 from an existing national monument and a U.S. Forest Service Scenic Area, encompasses surprising diversity. Within the boundaries of Nevada's only national park lie the state's highest mountain, 13,063-foot Wheeler Peak, a stand of bristle-cone pines that are among the oldest trees in North America, a glacier, and Lehman Caves, one of the most richly decorated caves in the country.

Rising from arid sagebrush desert to windswept alpine ridges, Great Basin National Park straddles the Snake Range, one of the highest mountain ranges in its region. Like the rest of the region, this landscape was shaped by colliding crustal plates: first pushed upwards 70 to 50 million years ago (while the adjacent Colorado Plateau, stiffened by its thick layers of sandstone, remained relatively level and undeformed), then, beginning 20 million years ago, stretched apart until the crust cracked in long north-south-trending faults. Some blocks of crust sank, becoming today's basins; others tilted and floated, becoming mountain ranges.

The Snake Range forms a classic mountain "island," its heights snagging precipitation that never reaches the basin floors. This relatively cool, wet refuge shelters animals and plants that could not survive in the desert, from elk to water shrews, aspen trees to columbines, and a small glacier left from 12,000 years ago, when many ice rivers flowed out of the high peaks in the Great Basin ranges. Other long-surviving relicts grow on the upper slopes of high peaks in the Snake Range: groves of bristlecone pines. These gnarled, wind-blasted forms are among the oldest trees known on earth. A grove on Wheeler Peak sheltered the oldest-known tree until 1964, when the 4,950-year-old bristlecone was cut down, despite public protest, so that a scientist could count its annual growth rings. The stout, many-branched trunks of these venerable pines are largely bare, their wood polished to marble smoothness by the constant wind, their few live branches sustained only by a thin strip of bark and vascular tissue.

Under the lower slopes of Wheeler Peak lies Lehman Caves, a quarter-mile-long cavern named for Absalom Lehman, a rancher and miner who promoted the cave as a tourist attraction in the late 1800s. Despite its small size, Lehman boasts a profusion of "decorations," cave formations built drip by drip by groundwater carrying dissolved limestone. Among the display are stalactites, stalagmites, flowstone, columns, draperies, and soda straws,

as well as rarer formations, including Lehman Caves' signature formation: shields, pairs of symmetrical disks separated by a hairline crack, like two halves of a clam shell, with stalactites and flowstone hanging from their edges.

Wheeler Peak Scenic Drive, a twelve-mile paved road leading from the park's Visitor Center to Wheeler Peak Campground at 9,886 feet, provides a cross-section of the park's diversity as it climbs from piñon pine–juniper woodlands through ponderosa pine forests, montane spruce-fir, and finally to mountain meadows near the upper treeline. Trails to the ancient bristlecone pine grove, the glacier, and the summit of Wheeler Peak begin from the scenic drive. The unpaved Baker Creek and Snake Creek roads lead to trails and campgrounds in the wilder, less-visited southern part of the park. Snow closes all three roads in winter. An easy three-quarter-mile walk on paved, lighted trails shows off the marvels of Lehman Caves. There's a lot to see in a country that appears bleak and forbidding, a place often seen only in the rear-view mirror.

–Susan J. Tweit

Wheeler Peak and Jeff Davis Peak in the Snake Range

Aspen frame Jeff Davis Peak at sunset.

Autumn snow near the summit of Wheeler Peak with Snake Valley in the distance

Rocky Mountain

"FOR SOME TIME WE WERE UNABLE TO DECIDE WHETHER what we saw were mountains," wrote Edwin James on June 30, 1820, as Major Stephen Long's expedition came within sight of the Front Range of the Rocky Mountains, "or banks of cumulus clouds skirting the horizon.... Towards evening the air became more clear, and...we could distinguish their grand outline, imprinted in bold indentations upon the luminous margin of the sky."

The Rockies are not North America's highest chain of mountains, but they are one of the most imposing, rising nearly two vertical miles from the Great Plains in places, in a wall visible from nearly a hundred miles away. They are also the longest, stretching nearly 10,000 miles from Canada to central Mexico. And the Rocky Mountains are North America's Great Divide: streams on the west side drain into the Pacific Ocean, streams on the east, into the Atlantic.

Rocky Mountain National Park, created in 1915, encompasses the "grand outline" the Long expedition spotted from far out on the Plains, including 14,225-foot-high Longs Peak, named for Major Long. Roughly square in shape and covering 415 square miles, this is a mountain park, boasting more than sixty peaks rising higher than 12,000 feet, and over a hundred square miles of alpine tundra.

The ascent from Estes Park, at 7,500 feet on the park's eastern edge, to the park's windswept heights, is akin to traveling a thousand miles north. Beginning in open forests of orange-barked ponderosa pine, the road climbs through dense groves of Douglas fir, dotted with patches of fire-dependent lodgepole pine and aspen. Still higher, where snow lingers into July and mosquitoes are legion and ravenous, are forests of subalpine fir and Engelmann spruce. At upper treeline, between 10,000 and 11,500 feet, the constant wind prunes limber pine, fir, and spruce into dwarf forests of krummholz ("crooked wood").

Above the treeline lies the rolling alpine tundra, a world of plants no more than a few inches tall. These miniature lives hug the ground to absorb warmth from the sun-heated soil and find shelter from the desiccating wind. (With winds clocked as high as 201 miles per hour, Rocky Mountain is one of the windiest places on the continent.) Limited by a growing season as short as six weeks, tundra plants grow slowly—a moss campion a few inches across, for instance, may be 200 years old. Harsh and wind-whipped as it may be, the tundra explodes with life during its brief summer. Look for ebony-colored Magdalena alpine butterflies sunning on rockslides, and listen for the shrill whistles of pika, tiny rabbit relatives that harvest tundra plants for winter food.

U.S. Highway 34, or Trail Ridge Road, is the highest paved highway in the United States. From late May to mid-October, visitors take this route across the park from east to west, crossing the Continental Divide and passing through miles of tundra at elevations over 12,000 feet. The spiderweb of 350 miles of hiking trails in the park includes everything from easy strolls off Trail Ridge Road to multiday trips.

Keeping Rocky Mountain National Park wild is the Park Service's current challenge. Located just a two hour-drive from the Denver metropolitan area, the park hosts more than 3 million visitors each year. Most drive Trail Ridge Road, where traffic can peak at 700 cars an hour on busy summer weekends. To escape the crowds, drive one-way Old Fall River Road (also open only in summer) instead. This narrow, unpaved route runs along the cascades of Fall River, then switchbacks up the headwall of a glacier-carved cirque onto the tundra, where it meets Trail Ridge Road near the Alpine Visitor Center. Or hike a trail on the less-visited west side of the park, such as the seven-mile-roundtrip climb to Devil's Staircase, a ridge offering spectacular views of western Colorado.

—Susan J. Tweit

RIGHT: **Longs Peak, viewed from Trail Ridge Road, towers above windblown snow and clouds.**

BELOW: **Sprague Lake**

Ice-covered pine frames Mummy Range >>>

Grand Teton

APPROACHING GRAND TETON NATIONAL PARK FROM the east, travelers round a curve and are confronted by a breathtaking view: a wall of jagged peaks, seemingly close enough to touch, rises straight out of a level, green valley. Rising to heights above 13,000 feet, with bare rock faces and glacier-chiseled crags, the mountains are the Teton Range; the valley, scribed by the lazy loops of the Snake River, is Jackson Hole.

In the early 1800s French fur trappers viewing the range from its gentle, western slope saw a resemblance to three rounded breasts and christened the mountains *Les Trois Tétons*. Dude ranches and other tourist businesses sprang up in the early 1900s to capitalize on the spectacular scenery, but Jackson Hole residents resisted the establishment of Grand Teton National Park until 1929, nearly half a century after its neighbor to the north, Yellowstone, was set aside. Thanks in part to a gift of more than 33,000 acres of the valley by John D. Rockefeller, Jr., the park today takes in 485 square miles of the Teton Range and Jackson Hole, reaching from the south edge of Yellowstone nearly to the town of Jackson.

The story of Grand Teton's dramatic scenery is a tale of intrusion, immersion, explosion, uplift, and glaciation. Although its core is comprised of 2.5-billion-year-old rocks, overlain by layers of sea-floor sediments deposited over millions of years, the Teton Range itself is a youngster, a mere 5 to 9 million years old. Long after the rest of the Rockies were thrust up beginning some 55 million years ago, and long after the Yellowstone caldera exploded several times, blanketing the entire region in ash and lava, massive faulting wrenched the Tetons into being.

The Teton Range more than made up for its late start, however, by its dramatic vertical displacement. Rock layers in the still-rising mountains are as much as 30,000 feet higher than their equivalents, buried deep beneath the still-sinking floor of Jackson Hole. In the past

million years, ten pulses of glaciation carved the peaks into their distinctive craggy shape, gouging the deep U-shaped canyons that divide them and depositing mounds of glacial debris, called moraines, at the canyon mouths, which helped create the string of lakes at the base of the range.

Despite being peppered with inholdings of private land and encompassing a commercial jet airport, Grand Teton National Park remains wild. Earthquakes and wildfires still shape its breathtaking landscape, home to as many species of wildlife as Yellowstone, from enormous bison and gangly moose to tiny calliope hummingbirds and dung beetles.

Most of the park's 4 million annual visitors arrive in summer, when the roads and 200-plus miles of trails are free of snow. To escape the crowds, take a raft trip down the Snake River where it winds through Jackson Hole, floating in a leisurely fashion past the face of the Tetons, with views of nesting bald eagles, ospreys, and trumpeter swans. Or hike one of the quieter canyons in the southern part of the park, such as Granite Canyon, where hikers can ride the Teton Village tram to the top of Rendezvous Mountain, then hike downhill through flower-filled meadows. Or visit the Gros Ventre Slide, on the east edge of Jackson Hole, a testament to the power of ongoing geologic forces. In 1925, 75 million tons of rock, loosed by earthquakes and greased by rain, plunged downhill and partway up the opposite slope, damming the Gros Ventre River.

Author and climbing guide Jack Turner reports in his 1996 book *The Abstract Wild* that he has spotted flocks of white pelicans soaring—looping and wheeling in the intense blue sky—a mile in the air over the summit of 13,770-foot Grand Teton, the highest peak in the range. What takes these birds so high, and so far out of their way? Ecstasy, Turner concludes, the same sort of joy that inspires climbers to sing and yodel atop mountain summits. Amidst mountains so magnificent, why should humans have a monopoly on joy?

—Susan J. Tweit

Mt. Teton

Foldout: **Tetons reflected in Jackson Lake**

Cascade Creek and Mt. Owen

Yellowstone

WHEN FUR TRAPPER JOHN COLTER RETURNED FROM A trip through what is now northwest Wyoming in 1808 with reports of spouting geysers and boiling springs, he was dismissed as a teller of tall tales. Other travelers, however, soon corroborated his stories. Joe Meek, for example, in 1829 looked over a ridge "and behold! the whole country beyond was smoking with vapor from boiling springs, and burning with gases issuing from small craters."

In 1871 geologist Ferdinand V. Hayden led a government expedition to document Yellowstone's wonders. The survey's report, illustrated by painter Thomas Moran and photographer William Henry Jackson, convinced Congress to create the world's first national park in 1872. The act set Yellowstone aside as a "pleasuring-ground for the benefit and enjoyment of the people," while ensuring the "preservation... of all timber, mineral deposits, natural curiosities, or wonders within." The U.S. Army patrolled the sprawling wilderness from 1886 to 1916 to enforce the law. The buildings at Fort Yellowstone, one of the best-preserved nineteenth-century calvary posts in existence, are still in use at Mammoth Hot Springs.

Within the roughly square boundaries of 3,440-square-mile Yellowstone National Park are a host of marvels, including more than over 10,000 thermal features—two-thirds of the world's geysers, as well as hot springs, mudpots, and fumaroles belching odoriferous gases; the 1,500-foot-deep Grand Canyon of the Yellowstone River, with two immense waterfalls, one twice the height of Niagara Falls; Yellowstone Lake, the largest high-altitude lake in North America; the 500-million-year-old fossil forest of Specimen Ridge (the inspiration for mountain man Jim Bridger's tales of petrified birds singing from petrified trees); and seven mountain ranges and high plateaus.

Yellowstone's world-class assemblage of thermal features stems from its location over a "hot spot" in the earth's mantle where molten rock comes as close as two miles below the surface (the usual depth is fifteen to thirty miles), heating groundwater beyond a boil. Once super-heated, the water squirts up to the surface through cracks in the rocks, exploding as geysers and mudpots, or burbling out as pools and springs. Algae and filamentous bacteria paint the edges of hot springs and streams with bright bands of color. The thermal features are most spectacular in the cooler air of dusk and dawn, when clouds of steam rise off hot pools and billow from geysers.

Often called the "American Serengeti," Yellowstone is home to at least 20,000 elk, several thousand American bison, some 250 grizzly bears, as well

Castle Geyser, Old Faithful Geyser Basin

Tourists at Old Faithful

as bighorn sheep, moose, deer, pronghorn, and a variety of other wildlife, including twenty-nine species of mosquitoes. Around a hundred gray wolves, exterminated in the 1930s and reintroduced in 1995 amidst much controversy, roam the park. Hayden Valley, in the central part of Yellowstone, is the single best place to watch wildlife. The wolves are most often seen in Lamar Valley, in the northeast corner of the park.

In the summer of 1988 a combination of drought, unusually high temperatures, and a hundred years of fire suppression spawned fires that burned nearly one million acres in and around Yellowstone. Despite predictions that the park was "destroyed," its fire-adapted ecosystems have recovered beautifully. Dense lodgepole pine forests were reborn as grassy, wildflower-studded openings; aspen groves sprouted where none had been seen in half a century. The fire-created diversity of habitats has benefited most wildlife species.

The park's 350 miles of roads (open to auto traffic May through early November, and to snowmobilers, cross-country skiers, and snowshoers the rest of the year) are often jammed in summer, because 99 percent of the 3 million visitors never venture farther than a half mile from a road. A hike on one of Yellowstone's 1,100 miles of trails takes visitors into the heart of this sprawling wilderness to listen to the "whoosh" of a geyser erupting, watch the pelicans dive for fish in Yellowstone Lake, smell the nose-tickling fragrance of sagebrush after a summer rain, and to experience the magic of America's first national park.

—Susan J. Tweit

Lodgepole pine at Cupid Spring

Boardwalks at Minerva Terrace allow visitors
to get a good look at the formations

TOP RIGHT: **Hot pool boiling along the Firehole River, Upper Geyser Basin**

FAR RIGHT: **The river plunges over Yellowstone Falls into the Grand Canyon of the Yellowstone**

BELOW: **Shoshone Lake**

Waterton/Glacier

DRAMATIC MOUNTAIN SCENERY COEXISTS WITH NORTH America's most feared carnivores, the grizzly bear and timber wolf, at Waterton/Glacier. This International Peace Park was created in 1932 to recognize the natural unity of the two parks and the bonds of peace and friendship between Canada and the United States. Naturalist John Muir called this section of the northern Rockies "the best care-killing scenery on the continent." Slightly smaller than the state of Delaware, the combined park totals 1,700 square miles, more than 95 percent of which is on the U.S. side of the border. Though the parks are managed separately, the staffs collaborate on many fronts, including wildlife research and visitor information and protection. Both parks were designated International Biosphere Reserves and World Heritage Sites in 1995.

The raw ingredients of the park's extraordinary landscape were laid down as horizontal sediments in the ocean about one billion years ago. After these materials gradually hardened into limestone, mudstone, and sandstone, they were bent, folded, and fractured by mountain-building forces. Next, pressures from the west forced a 300-mile-long slab, now known as the Lewis Overthrust, over the rocks to the east. Finally, glacier ice and running water sculpted the raw materials into horns, spires, knife-edge ridges, and U-shaped valleys, bejeweling the landscape with hundreds of lakes.

Glacier occupies a special place on the Continental Divide: A raindrop falling on the summit of Triple Divide Peak could end up in the Pacific Ocean via the Columbia River system, in the Gulf of Mexico via the Missouri-Mississippi River systems, or in Canada's Hudson's Bay via the Athabasca River system. By intercepting moist air moving east from the Pacific on the western slope and creating a rain shadow on the eastern slope, the Livingston and Lewis ranges increase the habitat variation. Dense forests of larch, spruce, fir, lodgepole pine, and in some places western redcedar and hemlock cloak the western slopes, while grasses and aspen groves mark the east. The Overthrust compresses a wide variety of habitats into a relatively small area. As a result, Glacier has more than 1,000 plant species, sixty species of native mammals, and 200 species of birds, unusually high numbers for an area of its size. Alpine meadows teem with wildflowers during July and August when the last of the winter snows finally melt.

Glacier's most famous wildlife is its 300 grizzly bears, which comprise about one-third of the population remaining in the Lower 48 states. Wolves moving south out of Canada began re-establishing themselves in Glacier in the 1970s. Because of the abrupt climatic change from west to east, Glacier is the only U.S. national park outside Alaska to have both mountain goat and bighorn sheep.

The free-roaming herds of bison were gone by the time Waterton was set aside in 1895, and Glacier in 1910, but Wapiti, or Rocky Mountain elk, and moose abound.

Most of the two million annual visitors arrive in July and August, when all the roads are open including the Going to the Sun Road between Saint Mary Lake on the east side and Lake McDonald on the west. The park's lakes and streams afford excellent fishing, and excursion boat cruises are available at Many Glacier, Rising Sun, Waterton Lake, Two Medicine, and Lake McDonald. More than 800 miles of trails offer opportunities to avoid crowds. Avid birdwatchers visit the park each fall to watch more than 400 bald eagles congregate at Lake McDonald. From November through May, snowshoers, cross-country skiers, and snowmachiners have the park to themselves.

—Mike Macy

St. Mary Lake in Glacier National Park

Bear grass at Grinnell Lake

North Cascades

MOVED BY THE ALPINE BEAUTY OF THE NORTH CASCADE mountains, Henry Custer of the International Boundary Commission wrote in 1859, "Nowhere do the mountain masses and peaks present such strange, fantastic, dauntless, and startling outlines as here." Established in 1968, North Cascades consists of two park units and two National Recreation Areas. Separating the park into north and south units, Ross Lake National Recreation Area follows the Skagit River and includes two smaller lakes, three hydropower dams, the North Cascades highway, and most of the visitor facilities. Lake Chelan National Recreation area adjoins the south unit of the National Park. The four units total 1,068 square miles, an area slightly larger than Rhode Island, and are almost completely surrounded by U.S. Forest Service wilderness areas and British Columbia's Manning Provincial Park.

In 1916 mountain climber Laurie R. Frazier wrote, "On that day, we had our best view of the great old crag-turreted Shuksan. But the gigantic crawling glaciers scarred with seracs and mighty crevasses which lay between the dark frowning cleavers and the slender sheer pinacle girt with swirling cloud held out little room for encouragement. It seemed invulnerable." Though Frazier was describing what is now the park's highest peak, 9,131-foot Mt. Shuksan, her words echoed many early descriptions of the North Cascades—the most rugged part of the Cascade Range, which runs from Canada to northern California. The park contains none of the range's volcanos (the closest, Mount Baker is less than five miles from the north unit), but it does have hundreds of the waterfalls for which the range was named. Up to 110 inches of precipitation annually drench the west side of the park, nurturing temperate rain forests similar to those found along the Pacific Coast from Oregon to Alaska. Forest species include red alder, vine and big leaf maple, stinging nettles, devils club, Sitka spruce, Douglas fir, and Western hemlock and redcedar. A rain shadow with as little as thirty-five inches of precipitation annually accounts for the sagebrush meadows and ponderosa and lodgepole pine forests east of the Cascade crest. At higher elevations, much of the precipitation falls as snow, feeding the park's 350 alpine glaciers, more than half of those found in the Lower 48 states. Today's glaciers are remnants of those which carved many of the U-shaped valleys, including the Stehekin and Lake Chelan, one of America's deepest lakes. The bottom of this 1,500-foot-deep lake is some 400 feet below sea level, a reminder of the quarrying power of glaciers. North Cascade's varying precipitation and altitude create unusual botanical diversity; the park is home to more than 1,500 species of plants. North

Cascades is the only place in the Pacific Northwest frequented by both grizzly bear and timber wolves, immigrants from Canada re-establishing themselves south of the border.

North Cascades is just a three-hour drive from Seattle, but only about 23,000 visitors reach the park, which is penetrated by one narrow, windy road. More than 330,000 visit Ross Lake National Recreation area via the North Cascades Highway, which has been dubbed Washington's "most scenic." Closed during winter, the Highway provides several views into the park. There's no road to the historic resort of Stehekin at the head of Lake Chelan; though it's possible to hike or fly in, most Stehekin visitors arrive by boat, a fifty-five-mile voyage up the lake from the town of Chelan. Downed timber, thickets, and steep terrain made travel in the Cascades a nightmare before hundreds of miles of trails were built.

—Mike Macy

Mt. Challenger

Whatcom Peak from Tapto Lakes Basin

Mt. Shuksan reflects in Mirror Lake.

Wrangell-St. Elias

IN JULY 1741, AFTER WANDERING EASTWARD ACROSS the North Pacific from Siberia for six weeks, the explorer Vitus Bering declared that a cloudlike mass shimmering on the northern horizon was in fact a mountain. The predominantly Russian expedition had found North America and the world's highest coastal summit: 18,008-foot Mt. St. Elias stands a mere ten miles from tidewater at the junction between what is now Alaska's panhandle and the rest of the state. The explorers reached the coast and named the peak on St. Elias' Day, on the Russian Orthodox calendar.

Named a World Heritage Site in 1979 and designated a national park in 1980, Wrangell-St. Elias is the U.S.'s largest park. At more than 20,000 square miles, it is six times the size of Yellowstone, and larger than New Hampshire and Vermont combined. The park's name refers to its two loftiest mountain ranges. The St. Elias, higher of the two, is in the southeastern portion of the park, which is indented by Yakutat and Icy bays. Both bays terminate in fjords frequented by cruise ships during the summer. Between the two bays sprawls Malaspina Glacier, which covers an area larger than Rhode Island and was named for the Italian explorer who in 1791 was the first European to enter Yakutat Bay. Malaspina is one of the world's largest piedmont glaciers, that is, a solid compacted river of ice that has emerged from the mountains and spread over a broad, lowland plain. The lower range, the Wrangells, lies to the northwest of the St. Elias and includes four glaciated volcanoes that rise to 16,000 feet. Of these, only Mt.

Wrangell remains active, although it last erupted in 1900. At their northwest end, the Wrangells terminate abruptly along the Copper River, providing stunning views to motorists. A third range, the Chugach, roughly parallels the Wrangells west of the Chitina River valley, which is the primary land route into the park.

Most of the remainder of the park is accessible only to mountaineers and river runners, and for good reason. In 1891 I.C. Russell, one of the first to gaze into the heart of what is now the park, described what he saw from the shoulder of Mt. St. Elias: "I expected . . . a comparatively low, forested country. . . .What met my astonished gaze was a vast snow-covered region, limitless in expanse, through which hundreds, perhaps thousands of bare, angular mountain peaks projected. There was not a stream, not a lake, not a vestige of vegetation in sight. A more desolate or utterly lifeless land one never beheld." Snow and ice dominate here more than anywhere on the globe outside the polar regions and Greenland. Flightseeing is one way to recreate Russell's experience of this vast, indomitable landscape, which encompasses seventy-five named glaciers including the Bagley Icefield, the longest and largest valley glacier in North America.

Thanks to the predominance of snow and ice, the region has proven almost immune to settlement and exploitation. The primary exception followed the 1908 discovery of copper deep in the heart of the Wrangells. To extract the ore, a 150-mile long railroad was constructed from Cordova on the eastern edge of Prince

William Sound to Kennicott. Closed abruptly in 1938 and never reopened, the mine is the primary destination of most visitors who reach it by driving sixty-two miles on the bed of the abandoned railroad to the village of McCarthy, in the mountainous core of the park.

Varied habitat accounts for a dazzling diversity of wildlife in Wrangell-St. Elias. Whales and other marine mammals cruise its southern shores under the watchful eyes of mountain goat, bald eagle, and peregrine falcon. Inland, salmon course up the rivers while Dall sheep negotiate 7,000-foot ridges in search of food and refuge from predators. Moose, brown and black bear, wolves, and the occasional caribou and bison stalk the timbered valleys and sub-alpine slopes. Wrangell-St. Elias marks one of the southernmost nesting places for bird species commonly associated with arctic and interior Alaska.

—Mike Macy

RIGHT: **Mt. St. Elias from Kageat Point, Icy Bay**

BELOW: **Malaspina Glacier with Mt. St. Elias and Agassiz Lake**

Hiker overlooking Bagley icefield

Mt. Drum and the
Copper River

Glacier Bay

WHEN LIEUTENANTS WHIDBEY AND LE MESURIER became the first Europeans to reach this area while exploring Alaska's coast with Captain George Vancouver for the British Royal Navy in 1794, all of Glacier Bay was still under construction. They reported that the entrance was "terminated by compact solid mountains of ice, rising perpendicularly from the water's edge..." In other words, a mere 200 years ago, there was essentially no Glacier Bay. The core of what is now Glacier Bay National Park was covered by a glacier up to 4,000 feet thick, twenty miles wide, and seventy-five miles long, and the waters in front of the glacier were so clogged with freshly calved ice that it was all the explorers could do to squeeze past.

When naturalist John Muir arrived seventy-five years later, the ice had already retreated nearly forty-five miles northward. Muir found a landscape emerging from under the ice as he watched. Here, in 1879, was living proof that the dramatic landscape of his beloved Yosemite had indeed been carved by glaciers: "We saw the world-shaping forces at work; we scrambled over plains they [glaciers] had built but yesterday." Although the rate of retreat has since slowed, Glacier Bay is a sprawling complex of fjords extending some sixty-five miles into the Fairweather-St.Elias Mountains. Global climate change occasioned much of the glacial retreat, though cataclysms, particularly the giant earthquakes of 1899, also contributed.

Thanks in part to Muir's writings and sketches, Glacier Bay had become a tourist destination by 1900. To protect its scientific and scenic values, Glacier Bay was named a national monument in 1925. In 1980 it was designated a national park and enlarged by 58,406 acres around Dry Bay in the northwest sector. UNESCO named it a Biosphere Reserve in 1986 and a World Heritage Site in 1992. The only national park in Alaska which includes marine waters, Glacier Bay totals 5,125 square miles, an area slightly larger than Connecticut.

Glacier Bay, which is itself an enormous body of water, occupies the northern end of Southeast Alaska's labyrinthine Inside Passage and dominates the eastern half of the park. About twenty-five miles north of the entrance, the Bay divides into the Muir Inlet fjord complex on the north and the longer West Arm fjord complex to the northwest. On a clear day, John Hopkins Inlet is particularly spectacular because the adjacent peaks soar to 8,000 feet. The Fairweather Range, with 15,320-foot Mt. Fairweather, fifteen miles from the Pacific Ocean, dominates the western half of the park. The second-highest coastal range in the world, the Fairweathers intercept moisture from storms that roll in almost continuously off the Gulf. Falling mostly as snow, this moisture feeds the park's glaciers.

The park includes two other important but seldom-visited terrains that provide habitat and migration corridors for bears, wolves, goats, and other terrestrial wildlife. The southwest corner includes a number of bays and timbered headlands bordering Cross Sound and the Gulf of Alaska. The northwest corner consists of a narrow forested foreland fronting the tumultuous Gulf of Alaska and the Alsek River. The large estuary at the mouth of the Alsek provides an important staging area for migratory waterfowl and shorebirds. Strong currents and surf, an absence of visitor facilities, and the high cost of chartering vessels and aircraft discourage visitors.

Today, Glacier Bay remains one of the best places in the world to study glacial retreat and plant succession.

Where Vancouver's lieutenants saw only ice, there are now temperate rain forests of Sitka spruce with the oldest specimens more than two hundred years old. Wildlife has colonized the new forests and wetlands. During summer when the icebergs make ideal platforms for seal pups, the Bay teams with more than 4,000 harbor seals. When winds are calm, the blowing and thunderous breaching of humpback whales that migrate between Alaska and Hawaii can be heard mingling with the cries of coyote, wolf, geese, eagles, seabirds, and songbirds.

—Mike Macy

Opposite left: **Rain forest of Sitka spruce and western hemlock at Bartlett Cove.**

Opposite right: **Fairweather Range is reflected in one of the many lakes and ponds in the area.**

Below left: **Confluence of Alsek and Tatshenshini Rivers**

Below: **In this aerial view of Glacier Bay, Blue Pond, White Thunder Ridge, and Riggs Glacier are landmarks.**

Denali

ON THE MAPS, IT'S CALLED MT. MCKINLEY, AFTER THE late senator from Ohio who became the twenty-fifth President of the United States, but most Alaskans know North America's highest summit by its Athabascan Indian name, Denali, or The Great One. By any measure, it is great. At 20,320 feet, Denali lords over the rest of the Alaska Range, dwarfing even its closest rival, 17,400-foot Mt. Foraker, which Athabascans considered Denali's "wife." Denali towers 18,000 feet above the countryside immediately to the north. By comparison, the summit of Mt. Everest rises only 15,000 feet above the adjacent Tibetan Plateau. On clear days, the elephantine mass of Denali looms over Fairbanks, 160 miles to the north, and Anchorage, 135 miles to the south. Owing to its bulk, height, and location, Mt. McKinley is Alaska's centerpiece.

The mountain also functions as a beacon for Alaska's most popular national park, which draws more than 550,000 visitors per year. The tireless efforts of big game hunter Charles Sheldon and the Boone & Crockett Club led to the creation of Mt. McKinley National Park in 1917. Four million acres were added in 1980 to the original two million and the name was changed to Denali National Park and Preserve. The additions protect the mountain's summit and southern approaches and important wildlife habitat on the south slope of the Alaska Range, all of which were outside the original boundary. At 9,418 square miles, the park and preserve, which was made a World Biosphere Reserve in 1976, is larger than Vermont. Adolph Murie, the naturalist, wrote that even without the mountain (McKinley), the park "would be outstanding because of its alpine scenery, its arctic vegetation, and its wildlife. I have walked over the green, flowering slopes in the rain when the fog hid the landscape beyond a few hundred yards and felt that the white mountain avens, the purple rhododendrons, and the delicate white bells of heather at my feet were alone worthy of our efforts" (to protect the park). In addition to its sublime alpine scenery, Denali is home to more than 650 species of flowering plants. Because of the extraordinary diversity of wildilfe that inhabits the park, Denali is also considered the Yellowstone of the North. Grizzly bears, wolf, fox, Dall sheep, moose, caribou, ptarmigan, and birds of prey are relatively easy to see in the tundra and taiga. A dirt road, which winds ninety miles into Denali from the Parks Highway to the mining community of Kantishna, offers some of the best wildlife viewing in Alaska. To protect the animals, motorized access is restricted to buses and shuttle vans. The 180-mile round-trip tour to Wonder Lake at the foot of Mt. McKinley typically consumes twelve hours. Visitors wishing to linger can camp in one of several campgrounds along the road. Trails are few; the best hiking is along gravel bars and on ridges.

Climbers come from around the world to challenge Denali. For many, Denali is the ultimate goal; for others, the mountain is a training ground for the Himalaya. On a nice day, from a distance, Denali may look ripe for the picking, but summiting it and returning safely requires years of experience, months of conditioning, weeks of hard work on the mountain in brutal conditions, and considerable luck. Half of those who attempt Denali are stopped by altitude, frostbite, and weather. Even in summer, temperatures on the mountain drop to -35° F.

With winds frequently exceeding fifty miles per hour, windchills of -50° to -70°F are the norm. Because the earth's atmosphere thins toward the poles, the summit of Denali contains about as much oxygen as a Himalayan summit several thousand feet higher. Several of the published accounts of Denali climbs are classics of mountaineering literature. In the course of traveling 10,000 miles by dogsled as Archdeacon of the Episcopal Ministries in Alaska, Hudson Stuck determined that he "would rather climb that mountain than discover the richest gold-mine in Alaska." A member of the first party to climb Denali, Stuck wrote of the view from the summit, "What infinite tangle of mountain ranges filled the whole scene, until gray sky, gray mountain, and gray sea merged in the ultimate distance." And of that experience in 1913, he wrote, "I remember no day in my life so full of toil, distress, and exhaustion, and yet so full of happiness and keen gratification."

—Mike Macy

Mt. Foraker, Alaska Range

**Mt. McKinley and Reflection Lake
in the evening light of summer**

Mt. McKinley

Tundra and mountains viewed from above Polychrome Pass

Kenai Fjords

AFTER SEEING WHAT IS NOW KENAI FJORDS IN 1899, newspaper magnate Henry Gannett wrote, "The Alaska coast is to become the showplace of the earth, and pilgrims, not only from the United States, but from far beyond the seas, will throng in endless processions to see it." The throngs aren't endless yet, but in other respects Gannett was right: visitation at Kenai Fjords is growing faster than at any other national park in Alaska. There are three reasons for Kenai Fjords popularity: scenery, wildlife, and accessibility. Fjords are long, narrow, glacially carved inlets of the sea bounded by steep mountains; the park's fjords are exemplary, rarely more than a few miles wide, up to twenty-three miles long, and over 1,000 feet deep, bounded by snow and glacier-capped ridges more than 4,000 feet high. Kenai Fjords has the kind of marine and terrestrial wildlife one would hope to find in Alaska, and it lies 130 miles by road from Anchorage, Alaska's largest city.

The park sits on the east side of the Kenai Peninsula, about 100 miles west of the boundary between two tectonic plates. The Pacific Plate is moving slowly northwest and plunging under the Alaskan Plate at the rate of several inches per decade, producing Kenai Fjords' distinctive scenery: as the Pacific Plate plunges, it pulls the leading edge of the Alaska Plate down with it, submerging the east side of the Kenai Peninsula. The process is both continuous—averaging inches per decade—and occasionally cataclysmic—during the great Alaskan earthquake of 1964, the land in Kenai Fjords dropped six feet in a few seconds.

Glaciers have also played an important role in shaping this landscape, which is very much a work in progress—the retreat of Northwest Glacier between 1910 and 1950 left a new lagoon more than nine miles long. The 300-square-mile Harding Icefield crowns the northeastern portion of the Kenai Peninsula with ice up to one mile thick. The Harding and adjacent icefields feed seven major glaciers, which calve into or terminate within a few miles of the Gulf of Alaska. These glaciers and their antecedents have carved six major fjords, such as twenty-three-mile-long McCarty Fjord, and a score of lesser bays along the Peninsula's eastern edge. Many of today's smaller bays were originally cirques, or steep-walled, circular basins carved by alpine glaciers hundreds or thousands of feet above sea level; now they are drowned, providing habitat for fish and marine mammals. The combination of recent glaciation and active subsidence has created a landscape of extremely vertical yet often round-topped peninsulas and egg-shaped islands pounded almost continuously by large swells from the far corners of the Pacific. Flat land and beaches are rare.

The park's wildlife is equally impressive. Mountain goats lend a sense of scale to vertical mountainsides and add new meaning to the expression sure-footed. Numerous cliffs provide nesting sites for clouds of horned and common puffins, guillemots, oystercatchers, murrelets, harlequins, gulls, kittiwakes, and terns. Humpback, killer, fin, and gray whales; harbor seals, sea lions, porpoise, moose, and brown and black bear are frequently seen. Elsewhere sea otters are often shy and retiring, but in Kenai Fjords, they play and nap in full view of the tour vessels.

At just over 900 square miles, Kenai Fjords is the smallest of the national parks Congress created in Alaska in December 1980. Because of the steep terrain and lack of trails, Kenai Fjords offers few options for casual hiking. As a result, most of the 250,000 yearly visitors experience the park by tour boats and fishing charter vessels from Seward. For proficient sea kayakers and mountaineers, Kenai Fjords is a paradise.

—Mike Macy

BELOW LEFT: Icebergs calved from Ogive Glacier float in Northwestern Lagoon.

BELOW: Smoke drifts from volcanic Mt. Redoubt as sunset colors Cook Inlet.

OPPOSITE: Exit Glacier, Kenai Fjords

Lake Clark

LAKE CLARK NATIONAL PARK INCLUDES A GENEROUS sampling of much of the best that Alaska has to offer. John Kauffman, an advocate for the area's protection, wrote, "Think of all the splendors that bespeak Alaska: glaciers, volcanoes, alpine spires, wild rivers, lakes with grayling on the rise. Picture coasts feathered with countless seabirds. Imagine dense forest and far-sweeping tundra, herds of caribou, great roving bears. Now concentrate all these and more into less than one percent of the state — and behold the Lake Clark region, Alaska's epitome."

The 6,320-square-mile Lake Clark National Park and Preserve, created in 1980, is midway in size between Connecticut and New Jersey. In addition to the attributes mentioned by Mr. Kauffman, the park was created to protect the headwaters of the Kvichak River drainage, Alaska's most important sockeye, or red, salmon fishery. Each summer, hundreds of thousands of these spawning salmon provide an infusion of protein and energy for the park's wildlife and handful of residents.

Lake Clark, nearly fifty miles long, is by far the largest of several lakes on the west side of the park, which is about a hundred miles southwest of Anchorage. From prehistoric times, the lake and the Tlikakila River, which flows into it, provided one of the most important trading routes between Bristol Bay and Cook Inlet. But after living in the area for centuries, the Dean'ina Athabascan Indians began moving downriver to the villages of Nondalton and Iliamna about 100 years ago, shortly before trappers and prospectors began home-steading the region.

Two of Alaska's largest and most important mountain ranges, the Alaska and the Aleutian, meet in the park. The Chigmit Mountains occupy the park's core, and its peaks are among Alaska's most rugged. The active mountain-building and glaciation results from the collision of the Pacific and Alaska tectonic plates more than 150 miles to the east. The park sits over a critical juncture, precisely where the leading edge of the northwestward-moving Pacific Plate reaches melting depths as it dives under the Alaska Plate. The juncture is marked by the park's two active volcanoes, Mt. Redoubt and Mt. Iliamna. Redoubt erupted most recently, in 1966, but Mt. Iliamna has erupted at least six times in the last 330 years. Both of these heavily glaciated, ten-thousand footers loom over Cook Inlet, with Iliamna a mere ten miles inland. Although most of the glaciers that carved the park's lakes and valleys have retreated significantly, several are still more than ten miles long.

The park spans several ecosystems from coastal forest and wetlands through coastal mountain to interior forest. Tundra tidal flats, estuaries, and headlands fronting Cook Inlet provide habitat for shorebirds, waterfowl, and seabirds. Killer whale and the all-white beluga whale cruise just offshore. Recently, the Mulchatna caribou herd, which lives on the west side of the park, has mushroomed to some 300,000 animals, making it the state's second largest. In addition the park has wolf, wolverine, Dall sheep, moose, and beaver.

Only 12,000 people visit the park each year; virtually all come in the summer. Most visitors fly into Park Headquarters at Port Alsworth, either by charter or regularly scheduled commuter flights from Anchorage, Kenai, Homer, and Iliamna. Port Alsworth offers lodging and guide services. The park's three National Wild and Scenic Rivers are popular with rafters, but hiking is difficult, owing to the lack of trails, thick brush, numerous rivers, and steep terrain. Fishing—for red salmon and trophy rainbow and lake trout—can be excellent, though anglers may have to share the best fishing spots with brown bears. Former wilderness guide Bob Waldrop explained in the 1970s, "Something of most parts of Alaska is represented at Lake Clark, but more tersely. The Brooks Range and other Alaskan wilderness areas are elaborate novels; this is a poem." By Alaskan standards, Waldrop may be correct; but by practically any other measure, Lake Clark National Park and Preserve is an epic.

—Mike Macy

Autumn rainbow framing white spruces, willows, and dwarf birches along the shore of Lower Twin Lake

East end of upper Twin Lake, viewed >>> from the top of Falls Mountain

Gates of the Arctic

"NOTHING I HAD EVER SEEN...HAD GIVEN ME SUCH A sense of immensity as this virgin lake lying in a great cleft in the surface of the earth with mountain slopes and waterfalls tumbling from beyond the limits of visibility.... No sight or sound or smell or feeling even remotely hinted of men or their creations. It seemed as if all time had dropped away a million years and we were back in a primordial world. It was like discovering an unpeopled universe where only the laws of nature held sway." Bob Marshall, who wrote this testimonial to the pristine condition of the Central Brooks Range in his 1956 book, *Alaska Wilderness*, spent much of the decade between 1929 and 1939 exploring Alaska's northernmost mountain range and befriending local prospectors and Natives. The park takes its name from Marshall's descriptive term for a narrow section of the North Fork of the Koyukuk River that provides a mountain-lined corridor through the central Brooks Range into the treeless Arctic tundra fifteen miles upstream. Created in 1980 and named a World Biosphere Reserve in 1984, the park and preserve total 13,237 square miles and include the headwaters of six National Wild and Scenic Rivers.

The Brooks Range, the northernmost extension of the Rocky Mountains, runs 500 miles from east to west, dividing Interior Alaska from the North Slope. The park occupies the central portion of the range and offers stunning examples of extremely recent glaciation, although few glaciers remain today. The entire park is north of the Arctic Circle, but despite the high latitude and the length and intensity of the winter, the arid climate—precipitation averages around ten inches per year, less than that of San Diego—supports only a few remnant alpine glaciers.

A portion of the range of the Western Arctic caribou herd—currently Alaska's largest, at 400,000 animals—lies within the park. Wolves, wolverine, fox, and black and grizzly bear, moose, and Dall sheep are also seen frequently, in part because vegetation is so sparse. Timber consists of white spruce, black spruce, cottonwood, aspen, and willow on valley bottoms on the south slope of the range. To the north, trees are limited to shrublike alders and willows along stream banks and in gullies and a few adventurous cottonwood. Each summer about one hundred species of birds arrive from Europe, Asia, tropical archipelagos, and all over the Americas to join about twenty resident species in a short-lived cacophony of nesting and rearing.

There are no facilities inside the park, which receives only about 3,000 visitors per year. Access is by foot or charter aircraft after flying into Bettles or Anaktuvuk Pass or driving the Dalton Highway to Wiseman, 250 miles north of Fairbanks. There are no trails, and the hiking is grueling, although the park's tundra and gravel bars offer some of the best wilderness backpacking in Alaska. The granite-spired Arrigetch Peaks in the southwestern portion of the park attract climbers from around the world. Float trip options are unusually varied in length, scenery, and destination: north across the barren tundra to the Beaufort Sea, west through timber and tundra to the Chukchi Sea, or south into the heavily timbered Yukon River Basin. Most visitors come during June, July, and August, but winter has its beauty, too: low light paints landscape with pastel hues, river ice buckles into diamondlike domes ten feet tall; and sounds—of trees cracking, of thousands of ptarmigan conversing while grazing on willows, or wolves howling—carry for miles in the sub-zero cold. Cross-country skiing and dog-sled tours are best in early April. Visitors who want to experience the park's deep solitude should schedule time outside the two most popular areas, the Gates itself and the Arrigetch.

—Mike Macy

Two views of Matcharak Lake in the Noatak River region of Gates of the Arctic National Park

Katmai

KATMAI OWES ITS NATIONAL PARK AND PRESERVE STATUS to a big bang: in June 1912 Novarupta volcano on the flank of Mt. Katmai exploded. One of the four largest volcanic eruptions in recent history, it spewed out almost twice as much ash and cinders as the deadly Krakatoa eruption of 1883, enough to darken skies over most of the Northern Hemisphere. For two days, ash fell so heavily in the town of Kodiak, one hundred miles to the east, that it was impossible to see more than a few feet ahead. Fortunately, the Katmai area was unpopulated: the eruption, which is estimated to have had ten times the force of the 1980 eruption of Mt. St. Helens, left ash covering more than forty square miles around the volcano to depths of 700 feet! Only one eruption in the past 4,000 years—the 1500 B.C. eruption of Mt. Santorini in Greece—has displaced more volcanic material.

It was 1916 before anyone arrived to assess the effects of the eruption. The National Geographic Society expedition's leader Robert Griggs described what the ash flow looked like from Mt. Katmai that year: "The whole valley as far as the eye could see was full of hundreds, no thousands—literally, tens of thousands—of smokes curling up from its fissured floor." Although four years and three Alaskan winters had elapsed since the eruption, the expedition tallied 1,000 vents with steam still reaching 500 feet into the air and a few more with steam and smoke spiraling more than 1,000 feet into the atmosphere. "Our feeling of admiration soon gave way to one of stupefaction," Griggs recalled in 1917. "We were overawed. For awhile, we could neither think nor act in normal fashion. It was a situation calculated to instill dread."

Griggs named the area the Valley of the Ten Thousand Smokes and led the campaign to protect it. Set aside in 1918 as a national monument to protect the geologic moonscape, Katmai was expanded in 1980 when it was designated a national park and preserve, in part to protect the spawning grounds of the Naknek River sockeye salmon, one of Alaska's most important fisheries. Almost as large as the state of New Jersey, the 6,390-square mile park and preserve is on the Alaska Peninsula about 300 miles southwest of Anchorage. Today, the Valley of the 10,000 Smokes remains one of the prime attractions for the 55,000 people who visit Katmai each year. Time has since extinguished the 10,000 smokes, but any of the park's fifteen active volcanoes could roar to life at any time.

Another prime attraction that can roar to life at any time—and often does—is the park's coastal brown bear population. Weighing up to 900 pounds, these bears are the largest terrestrial carnivore on the planet. More than a score of them spend much of July and August fishing for sockeye salmon in the world-famous Brooks River between Brooks and Naknek Lakes—often in direct competition with humans who enjoy the sport. A raised observation platform provides a relatively safe, ringside seat. While best known for its bears, Katmai also offers moose, caribou, and wolves. The numerous lakes teem with swan, geese, ducks, shorebirds, and seabirds including the Arctic tern, which migrates 20,000 miles each year between Alaska and Antarctica.

Several air carriers offer daily flights from Anchorage to King Salmon, a short boat or float plane ride from Brooks Camp, the primary destination in the park. A twenty-three-mile long road runs from Brooks Camp to the Valley of 10,000 Smokes, and float planes provide access to other lakes. With so much space and the vast majority of visitors clustered at Brooks Camp and the adjacent lakes, Katmai offers myriad opportunities for solitude, especially along its wild coastal area like those fronting the Shelikof Strait. Thanks to Katmai's location between Bristol Bay and the Gulf of Alaska, however, visitors should be prepared for high winds and wet weather.

—Mike Macy

Brown bear and seagull fishing for salmon at Brooks Falls

Panoramic view of the Valley of 10,000 Smokes shows the
effects of one of the largest volcanic eruptions ever
recorded, which transformed this landscape in June 1912.

Kobuk Valley

MOST OF US TEND TO THINK OF WILDERNESS PARKS AS places untouched by people. Although Noatak River National Preserve, Cape Krusenstern National Preserve, and Kobuk Valley National Park include some of Alaska's most pristine wilderness, these three areas in northwest Alaska have been inhabited almost continuously for the past 5,000 years. All three areas were set aside as part of the Alaska National Interest Lands Conservation Act of 1980 and total 14,100 square miles, an area almost as large as New Hampshire and Vermont combined. On the east, Noatak National Preserve abuts Gates of the Arctic National Park; the resultant 18-million-acre complex is larger than West Virginia. Accessible mainly by charter aircraft, these are true wilderness areas, with no year-round ranger facilities, and no visitor facilities, roads, or trails. Collectively, the three areas receive about 12,000 visitors per year.

Kobuk Valley National Park includes a natural feature few associate with Alaska: a desert. The Great Kobuk Sand Dunes, the largest of the park's three dune fields, covers some twenty-five square miles. Formed at least 33,000 years ago by sand blown off glaciers in the Brooks Range and their outwash plains, the dunes come in all varieties, even barchans, the crescent-shaped dunes associated with the world's driest regions. During the last Ice Age, the Kobuk Valley was not glaciated, but the surrounding mountains were. This dry arctic steppe, or grassland, was ideal for grazing land animals and supported hunters whose ancestors had perfected their techniques on the steppes of Asia. Archaeological discoveries at Onion Portage show that people have lived on the Kobuk for at least 12,000 years, making it one of the oldest inhabited sites in the Americas. Sand and permafrost bluffs along the Kobuk River contain fossils of Ice Age horses, antelopes, bison, and mammoths. The climate changed about 9,000 years ago; forests began to

invade the grasslands, favoring browsers like moose and caribou. Today, Noatak Preserve and Kobuk Valley include part of the range of the Western Arctic caribou herd—currently Alaska's largest, at 400,000 animals.

Cape Krusenstern National Preserve, the westernmost of the three, fronts the Chukchi Sea and Kotzebue Sound. Every fifty to seventy-five years for the past 4,000 years, storms have added another gravel ridge to the beach front at the low-lying Cape. In response, Eskimo hunters moved their campsites a few yards seaward, leaving artifacts in their wake. As a result, 114 readily distinguishable beach ridges provide a nearly continuous record of Northwest Alaska's cultural evolution and preserve an anthropological treasure.

Noatak National Preserve, about twenty miles east of Cape Krusenstern, protects the upper 350 miles of the Noatak River, creating the largest mountain-ringed, wilderness drainage in the United States. It was designated a World Biosphere Reserve in 1976. S.B. McLenegan, an engineer on the *Corwin*, a U.S. Revenue steamer (the equivalent of today's Coast Guard cutters) was, in 1885, one of the first American visitors to the Noatak. He called it "one of the most desolate sections of country imaginable," but first impressions can be deceiving. While the lower valley is the treeless tundra one expects beyond the western limit of timber, the upper Noatak includes interior forests of black spruce, white spruce, birch, aspen, and cottonwood. Recent studies suggest that the Noatak drainage has 500 species of vascular plants, the greatest array of flora anywhere in the Far North. Desolate or not, people have lived in the Noatak, which means "passage to the interior," for at least the past 5,000 years. Given the harsh climate and dearth of construction materials and fuel, this achievement testifies to the technological sophistication of a "primitive" people.

—Mike Macy

Caribou tracks in the Great Kobuk Sand Dunes

OPPOSITE: **Sunrise over the Kobuk River at Onion Portage** >>>

Channel Islands

PORTUGUESE EXPLORER JOAO RODRIGUES CABRILHO was the first European to sight the Channel Islands, a loose cluster of eight islands off the coast of southern California, in 1542. After venturing as far north as Monterey Bay, Cabrilho and his fleet of two small, leaky ships returned to San Miguel in the Channel Islands, where the pioneering seafarer died of a gangrene infection from a broken arm.

Islands are not common on the Pacific Coast between the Strait of San Juan de Fuca and San Diego Bay; the Channel Islands are one of just two island clusters punctuating the entire coast. Isolated from the mainland by eleven to forty miles of ocean, the Channel Islands are visible from the crowded coast on clear days, but are worlds apart. Their uplands, sheltered valleys, beaches, and offshore waters abound with life, from blue whales, the world's largest mammals, to tiny island poppies, found nowhere else.

In 1980 the five northern islands, Anacapa, Santa Cruz, Santa Rosa, San Miguel, and Santa Barbara, were designated as Channel Islands National Park, the nation's fortieth park. Just half of the park's 390 square miles is terrestrial; the remainder is underwater, stretching one nautical mile into the ocean around each island.

This submerged landscape sustains one of the Channel Islands' marvels, "forests" of giant bladder kelp, algae whose slender, leafy stems stretch 150 or 200 feet from ocean bottom to the water's surface. These undersea groves, which sway gently with passing waves, rival tropical forests in their diversity and productivity. They provide homes, lunch counters, or trysting grounds for more than 750 species of fish and invertebrates, and for many mammals and birds as well. Sea otters, for instance, depend on the groves of giant seaweed for shelter, food, and nurseries; in turn, the otters dine on sea urchins, grazers which, if left unchecked, clearcut whole stands of the giant kelp.

In winter and spring thousands of northern elephant seals, California sea lions, northern fur seals, and other pinnipeds—flipper-footed mammals—haul out on the normally quiet beaches of the Channel Islands. These blubbery creatures sound a cacophony of bellowing and barking as males joust over females and the two sexes mate. Six species have been sighted at Point Bennett on San Miguel, making it the most diverse pinniped rookery in the world.

An unusual number of endemic species—plants and animals found nowhere else—inhabit the Channel Islands. Ten to 15 million years ago, the islands were attached to mainland Mexico. In the intervening millennia, movement along the San Andreas fault system has pushed the islands northwestward hundreds of miles to their current location. Isolated from the mainland for their long "voyage," the islands' resident plants and animals evolved into unique species. Sixty-five plant species are native only to the islands, ranging from the island oak, a tree reduced to shrub size, to the giant yellow coreopsis, a shrubby sunflower relative that can grow to the size of a small tree. Endemic animals include the cat-sized island fox, the island scrub jay, and the extinct pygmy mammoth.

Tools, butchered pygmy mammoth remains, and firepits show that humans have inhabited the Channel Islands for perhaps as long as 40,000 years. When Cabrilho stopped here, several thousand Chumash and Gabrieleño Indians lived on the larger islands. Since then, the islands have been home to sheep, cattle, and goat ranches, vineyards, olive orchards, movie companies, U.S. Navy bombing ranges, and Coast Guard lighthouses, resulting in serious disturbance to the native flora and fauna.

The Channel Islands can be reached only by boat; the most accessible trips, offered by the National Park concessionaire from its mainland headquarters in Ventura Harbor, range from several hours to most of the day. But travelers to these remote locations are rewarded by a rich and varied world of undersea kelp groves, feeding whales, bellowing pinnipeds, and blooming wildflowers, a reminder of the wondrous natural diversity that once characterized the southern California Coast.

—Susan J. Tweit

The last of the horses were removed from Santa Cruz Island in 1998 as part of the park service's efforts to restore the natural ecosystem. Anacapa Island is seen beyond.

TOP: Rocky shore on north side of Santa Barbara Island

ABOVE: Harbor seals frolic in the marine preserve off Santa Barbara Island

RIGHT: Anacapa Island

Death Valley

DEATH VALLEY WAS NAMED BY A PARTY OF FORTY-NINERS after they lost three members and twenty-eight of their twenty-nine wagons while taking a shortcut across this 120-mile-long desert basin in December 1849. By the 1920s the advent of the automobile made travel through this hot and harsh landscape less hazardous and tourists began to explore the area. In 1933 part of Death Valley became a national monument. In 1994 the California Desert Protection Act expanded it to 5,234 square miles and declared it a national park.

Death Valley is a desert's desert: rugged, forbidding, and almost unimaginably hot and dry. Elevations within the park range from 282 feet below sea level, the lowest point in the Western Hemisphere, just west of Badwater, to 11,331-foot-high Telescope Peak in the Panamint Mountains. This extreme range in elevations was created when movement in the earth's crustal plates stretched the crust under the region where Death Valley lies. As the crust stretched, faults tore it, dropping some sections down, tilting and floating others. The basin we call Death Valley sunk especially far; in fact, geologists say the actual floor is 8,000 to 9,000 feet below today's surface, buried under debris carried by the Amargosa River and the other streams that drain into this closed basin.

Lying in the rain shadow of the massive Sierra Nevada and encompassing the lowest elevations on the continent, the floor of Death Valley averages just 1.75 inches of rain a year, and holds the Western Hemisphere record for high temperature: 134° F on July 10, 1913 at Furnace Creek. Ground temperatures in summer routinely reach a searing 200° F, hence the Death Valley Shoshone Indians' name for the valley, *Tomesha*, or "Ground on Fire." That plants and animals manage to survive in this extreme landscape seems miraculous. Perhaps the most surprising of Death Valley's wild residents are desert pupfish, small fish named for their chubby physique and playful behavior. Unique to the area's isolated springs and streams, these fish are true desert-dwellers, able to survive in water as hot as 113° F, five times as salty as the ocean, and with dissolved oxygen concentrations that prove fatal to other gill-breathing fish.

Despite its brutal climate and sere landscape, humans have lived in Death Valley for at least the past 9,000 years. But people didn't make much of an impact until the late 1800s, when Forty-niners searched for fortunes among its bleak hillsides. Silver and gold strikes in the mountains around Death Valley spawned rich but short-lived boom towns such as Panamint City, Chloride City, Skidoo, Harrisburg, and Rhyolite. A more prosaic mineral, however, made Death Valley famous and led to its preservation: borax. Beginning in 1883, the Harmony Borax Works shipped 12 million tons of borax out of Death Valley on huge wagons pulled by hundred-foot-long, twenty-mule teams. A young man named Stephen T. Mather who worked as a publicist for the borax industry would later become the first director of the National Park Service and ensure the area's protection.

These days, travelers can whiz across Death Valley in a couple of hours. But the landscape that writer Mary Austin called "the loneliest land that ever came out of God's hands," in her paean to the California deserts published in 1903, *The Land of Little Rain*, is best experienced at a slower pace. Walk around the Harmony Borax Works, just north of the Visitor Center at Furnace Creek, to feel the trials of mining in these harsh conditions. Visit the salt pan at Devil's Golf Course to know the flat depths of the valley. Listen for the salt crystals cracking as they expand in the day's heat. Camp at remote Eureka Dunes to see a sky littered with stars and hear the wild coyote choruses. Or climb Telescope Peak into a world of ancient bristlecone pines and a dizzying view of Death Valley, 11,500 feet below. A visit to the valley of death reveals life's astonishing toughness and endurance.

—Susan J. Tweit

LEFT: A rare snow storm covered Joshua trees with rime ice and hoarfrost on the desert floor.

BELOW: The desert panorama from Dante's View includes the highest and lowest points in the park from Badwater to Telescope Peak.

Salt deposits on the valley floor at Devil's Golf Course

Sand dunes with Grapevine Mountains in distance

Telescope Peaks and the Panamint Range >>>
reflected in pool at Badwater

Reflection of El Capitán in the Merced River

ABOVE: **Half Dome and El Capitán, two of the iconic rock formations in the Yosemite Valley at twilight.**

<<< **Nevada and Vernal Falls viewed from the Panorama Trail at Glacier Point**

Joshua Tree

JOSHUA TREE NATIONAL MONUMENT WAS ESTABLISHED in 1936 after Minerva Hamilton Hoyt, a Los Angeles socialite, lobbied to protect the unique plants of this stretch of rocky landscape where the Mojave and Sonoran deserts meet. Although it originally included 825,000 acres, its size has waxed and waned. In 1950, mining interests induced Congress to remove 265,000 acres. When the California Desert Protection Act was passed in 1994, 234,000 acres were added back, bringing the total area to 793,000 acres, or 1,239 square miles, and the monument became Joshua Tree National Park.

Joshua trees, so the story goes, got their name in the 1800s when Mormons traveling through the Mojave Desert imagined that the twisting arms of the oddly shaped yuccas resembled the biblical prophet Joshua, pointing the way to the Promised Land. Growing up to thirty-five feet tall and sprouting multiple arms, these are the Southwest's largest yuccas, and with maximum lifespans of 1,000 years, rank among the desert's older plants. Just as saguaros are the

signature cacti of the Sonoran Desert, Joshua trees are the symbol of the Mojave Desert, growing at the higher elevations of this desert from southern California and southern Nevada to southwestern Utah and northwestern Arizona.

Also like saguaros, Joshua trees are the tallest plants in their landscape. Their sturdy forms provide homes, perches, and food for a variety of animals, from red-tailed hawks to pack rats, including some, like yucca night lizards, found nowhere else. These tiny, charcoal gray lizards spend their entire lives sheltered under the fallen trunks of dead Joshua trees, eating termites and ants, and are consumed in turn by owls and rattlesnakes.

Joshua Tree National Park spans the boundary between two deserts: its Joshua-tree-studded uplands are in the Mojave Desert, its lower, drier basins represent the western edge of the Sonoran Desert. Both are spare, sere landscapes. But if fall and winter bring rain, these seemingly barren expanses explode with life in early

spring. During the few weeks or months that the soil stays moist, annual wildflowers carpet the normally bare ground. These plants sprout, grow, bloom, and set seed in the brief period before the soil dries out, taking advantage of the ephemeral moisture. The boom in plants triggers a boom in animal lives as well: Costa's hummingbirds move in to nest and feed on nectar, endangered desert tortoises emerge from dormancy to graze, toads dig to the surface to sing and mate, insects hatch by the billions.

Joshua Tree National Park occupies a block of earth's crust raised above the surrounding landscape by two fault systems: the San Andreas on the south and the smaller Pinto Mountain Fault on the north. Springs issuing from these breaks in the crust once watered numerous groves of California fan palm, the largest palm native to the continental United States, and the tree for which Palm Springs and Palm Desert were named. Excessive groundwater pumping has killed most of these

green, shady oases, but a few remain inside the park, including Lost Palms, Cottonwood, and Fortynine Palms Oasis.

Eighty miles of paved roads, more than one hundred miles of dirt roads, and seventy miles of trails crisscross Joshua Tree National Park. Most visitors enter the park from its north side, and drive the thirty-mile main road through the higher parts of the park, passing through groves of queerly twisted Joshua trees and granite eroded into blocky, towering forms like piles of modern sculpture. The park's largest fan palm oasis, Lost Palms, a magical spot of water and green in the sun-bleached desert, hides down a seven-mile-roundtrip trail from Cottonwood Springs, near the park's southern entrance. The forty-mile paved road from Cottonwood Springs to the main park road climbs from the lowest elevations in the park to the highest, traversing the wide range of diversity contained in the word "desert."

—Susan J. Tweit

TOP: Joshua Tree National Park offers challenges to experienced rock-climbers.

FAR LEFT: Windblown sand rounded the form of this boulder, while water seeping into cracks created the fissured structure of many other rock formations in the park.

LEFT: Wildflowers brighten the desert landscape in spring.

Teddy bear cholla in Cholla Garden

Joshua trees beside granitic boulders at Belle Campground

Sequoia & Kings Canyon

THE HISTORY OF THESE TWO ADJOINING NATIONAL PARKS, which together protect 1,350 square miles of the spectacular Sierra Nevada, including the highest peak in the continental United States, 14,494-foot Mount Whitney, and the largest groves of giant sequoia trees, is the story of the ongoing conflict over exploitation versus preservation. In 1885, outraged by wholesale logging of the giant sequoias and unrestrained grazing of the mountain meadows, an unusual alliance—conservationists, the American Association for the Advancement of Science, and the Southern Pacific Railroad—began calling for a national park to protect the watersheds of the western Sierra. In September 1890 President Benjamin Harrison signed legislation creating America's second national park, Sequoia.

Any elation was short-lived, however: the park encompassed only 50,000 acres and despite its name, included no giant sequoias. A week later, Congress created tiny, 2,560-acre General Grant National Park, the forerunner of Kings Canyon, to safeguard two groves of sequoias, and tripled the size of brand-new Sequoia National Park. Still, neither park touched the high Sierra. Not until 1926 were the boundaries of Sequoia extended to the Sierra crest; in 1940, after intensive lobbying, Kings Canyon National Park was established, taking in the spectacular canyons of the Kings River country to the north of Sequoia, and the old General Grant National Park.

But the battle for the high Sierra was not over. The southern boundary of Sequoia was drawn with an enormous bite missing where Mineral King, an area of high peaks containing deposits of silver ore, had been omitted. In 1965 the Disney Corporation proposed a destination ski resort for Mineral King's high, wild basins. The Sierra Club took the project to court, and after a lengthy legal and public relations battle, Disney gave up. Mineral King was finally added to Sequoia in 1978, uniting the southern part of the park.

Most visitors come to Sequoia and Kings Canyon for the groves of giant sequoias, the largest living beings on earth. Although not as tall as coast redwoods, sequoias are far more massive: General Sherman, the largest-known sequoia, growing in Giant Forest at Sequoia National Park, weighs an estimated 1,385 tons. Its trunk is 275 feet tall and 102 feet around at the base; its first branch, nearly seven feet in diameter—the size of a large tree itself—takes off thirteen stories above the ground. An estimated 2,300 to 2,700 years old, this tree was already an adult when Christianity was born.

Once widespread across North America and Europe, sequoias' range shrank as climates warmed and dried over the past 60 million years. Today, they survive only along a 260-mile stretch of the Sierra Nevada between 5,000 and 7,000 feet elevation, watered by deep winter snows. These giants grow in a mixed conifer forest with other trees—white fir, sugar pine, yellow pine, and incense-cedar—all big trees themselves, but overshadowed by the sequoias.

Just two paved roads, Kings Canyon Highway and Generals Highway, both constructed in the early days of auto travel and thus narrow, winding, and not suitable for extra-long vehicles, lead into the lower edges of the two parks. Kings Canyon Highway, the only road into Kings Canyon, goes through Grant Grove, home of the second-largest sequoia, General Grant, then plunges down into Kings Canyon (winter snows close this part of the road), ending a few miles further at Road's End. Heavily traveled Generals Highway runs from Grant Grove in a loop through the lower elevations of Sequoia, passing several sequoia groves, including Giant Forest, home of General Sherman. The majority of both parks remain wild, accessible only by foot or on horseback. These vast vistas—mile upon mile of quiet mountain forests, jagged peaks, and bare granite basins cupping sapphire lakes—are the heart of the Sierra Nevada, a world conservationists fought for nearly a century to protect.

—Susan J. Tweit

OPPOSITE LEFT: **Upper Dusy Basin at Kings Canyon**

OPPOSITE RIGHT: **Lone Pine Peak in morning light, viewed from the Alabama Hills on the outskirts of Sequoia National Park**

ABOVE: **Moonset over Mt. Whitney**

RIGHT: **Sequoia bole and pines, redwood and moss-covered granite in Giant Forest**

Lassen Volcanic

BEFORE MOUNT SAINT HELENS STOLE ITS THUNDER IN 1980, Lassen Peak in northern California boasted the most recent volcanic eruption in the Lower 48. The spectacular event began in 1914 with a year of volcanic activity, and came to a head in May 1915 with a seven-mile-high eruption of ash and volcanic material, radically altering the landscape. The pyrotechnics earned Lassen National Park status in 1916, when President Theodore Roosevelt set aside both the peak and 106,000 acres around the juncture of the Sierra Nevada and Cascade Mountains. The rumble of volcanic activity continued for another five years. Lassen Peak, rising 2,000 feet to an elevation of 10,457 feet above sea level, is part of the Pacific Ring of Fire, a wheel of volcanic zones encircling the Pacific that often trigger earthquake activity where plates that compose the earth's crust collide.

Lassen emerged as a vent on the north side of Mount Tehama, now extinct and collapsed. The Earth has four types of volcanoes, based on types of lava, and examples of each are found in Lassen Volcanic National Park. Lassen Peak itself is a volcanic dome, specifically a plug-dome, when thick lava that had emerged from Tehama formed 27,000 years ago in less than a decade, cool plugged up its own vent. Stratovolcanoes, such as the remnants of Mount Tehama, are composites of thick lavas. Mount Harkness and West Prospect are shield volcanoes, spewing thin balsatic lava that spreads in broad sheets (Mauna Loa and Mauna Kea are famous examples). Cinder cones, the most common volcanic type, are formed by short eruptions of pea-to-walnut-sized lava rocks injected with gas and air, which stack themselves into steep-sided cones typically no higher than 1,000 feet. Lassen Park's best example is Cinder Cone, a starkly black, 800-foot pyramid that erupted in the eighteenth century. Although Lassen Peak is dormant, scientists believe it is one of the Cascade's peaks most likely to become active again. The geothermal area around it murmurs night and day—bubbling mud pots; steaming fumaroles; hot, sometimes boiling, springs; sulfur vents that emit a putrid odor. Sulphur Works, at the center of former Mount Tehama in the southwest corner of the park, is a hotbed of sulfurous activity, which can be viewed (and smelled) from a boardwalk that overlays the thin crust. Bumpass Hell—named for Kendall Bumpass who fell through the crust in 1864, seriously burning his legs—is an extensive tract of boiling pools and burbling mud pots.

But not all the tectonic phenomena are active. Chaos Jumbles, a collection of rocks and boulders strewn over four square miles, is the result of an avalanche 300 years ago that crashed down Chaos Crags and crossed the valley at speeds over 100 mph. The Devastated Area, the land where all vegetation was instantaneously eradicated in the 1915 eruption, is slowly rejuvenating itself.

Interspersed with the volcanic features are vast areas of the park where life flourishes. Lassen supports more than 700 species of plant life, and its meadows are flush with wildflowers from early summer until September.

One of the loveliest is Upper Meadow below Lassen Peak, dissected by Kings Creek. Alpine tundra and evergreen forests dip into stream-fed valleys.

Lassen National Park's visitor center is at the western entrance, a day's drive from San Francisco Bay. The park's 35-mile main road passes fir-lined Manzanita Lake in the northwest corner, skirts three sides of Lassen Peak, and leads to the trails, lakes, and geothermal areas. The park has 150 miles of trails. The Lassen Peak Trail attracts the most ambitious climbers for a five-hour (round-trip) hike into thin mountain air which carries the reward of magnificent views from the volcano's summit. Cinder Cone, in the more remote northeast corner of the park, is reached by a hike from Summit or Butte Lake. Fishing and boating are allowed on many of the lakes that dot the park. A winter sports area is near the southwest entrance.

—Susan Burke

Lassen Peak reflected in the waters of Manzanita Lake

Redwood

THE ONLY PRACTICAL WAY TO COMMUNE WITH A redwood, perhaps, is to lie flat on your back and cast your eyes up and up and up its trunk to the top of the tree some ten stories overhead. The *Sequoia sempervirens* (which earns its Latin sobriquet "everlasting" because it seems almost impervious to insects, disease, and wildfires), is a taller cousin of the giant sequoia, grows to 200 to 240 feet, and weighs hundreds of tons. For two centuries after 1769, when the redwood forests were first explored along the coast of northern California and Oregon by Fray Juan Crespi, they fell to a more persistent eradicator—profit—especially in the nineteenth century when logging began in earnest. Save-the-Redwoods League organized in 1918, and over the next fifty years with state financial help acquired large tracts of redwoods, totaling about 50,000 acres, which were added into the state park system. These ancient trees have life spans of 500 to 700 years—with some specimens known to have lived 2,000 years—but the logging continued and millions were being felled to build suburban decks and patio furniture. By 1965 an estimated two million original acres of forest were reduced to about 300,000 acres and counting. The possibility that the rest of this irreplaceable virgin forest could be eradicated led Congress to create Redwood National Park, a joint preservation effort that includes three California state parks—Prairie Creek, Del Norte Coast, and Jedediah Smith. The national park was enlarged in 1978, and now totals 106,000 acres, about 40,000 containing old-growth specimens at least 400 years old. Much of the new area, cut over by 1978, is now being rehabilitated with seeding, planting, and erosion control, propagating redwoods for the centuries ahead.

The towering trees, soaring out of the dark understory toward the sunny stratosphere, are the park's primary attraction. Their numbers include the tallest tree on earth, a 367.8-foot titan that is the centerpiece of Tall Trees Grove on the banks of Redwood Creek. The grove is aptly named, for the second-, third-, and sixth-tallest trees also reside there. The particular habitat required by these redwoods—moist sea air—is also a superb environment for visitors to the park. Coast redwoods, the popular name for this species, grow only within forty miles of the Pacific and flourish on this unspoiled coastline marked by dramatically steep and rocky cliffs. Pods of gray whales making their yearly migration between the Arctic and Baja are often sighted from Crescent Beach Overlook. Closer to shore, harbor seals, porpoises, and sea lions play. Sea birds account for half of the 300 species in the park.

The rich intertidal zone accommodates 168 species of invertebrates. The forest's dense understory hosts vinemaples, oaks, and alders, azaleas, huge rhododendron, and many kinds of ferns. Interspersed with the forests are prairies bright with wildflowers in the spring, home to roaming blacktail deer and coyote, along with mountain lions, bobcats, and the impressively antlered Roosevelt elk (which also frequents Gold Bluffs Beach, where the sand is laced with gold dust). Freshwater streams and rivers boast beaver and mink and otter, as well as the famous steelhead trout and salmon.

Redwood National Park is networked with trails that wind through redwood groves and spruce forests, along river bluffs and rugged ocean coastline. The driving is extraordinarily scenic (take turns at the wheel) on Klamath Beach Road, on U.S. 101 itself, and on unpaved roads through the redwood forests. In the summer, a soothing fog hovers almost daily, keeping the leaf surfaces moist and lubricating the redwoods' roots.

—Susan Burke

Coast redwoods thrive in fog-shrouded groves cooled by the wet winds blowing off the Pacific.

A panoramic-format camera turned to emphasize the height of the towering redwood trees.

Crater Lake

IF CRATER LAKE HAD BEEN CREATED ACCORDING TO A recipe, it might read something like this: 1) Build a large Cascade Range volcano (now known as Mt. Mazama) until its top is 13,000 feet above sea level. 2) Through a violent eruption, squeeze out Mt. Mazama's contents (some seventy-five cubic miles of material), leaving only the volcano's outer shell or roof. 3) Using gravity, punch down Mt. Mazama's now unsupported roof. 4) Seal any cracks in the floor of the resultant pie shell-like caldera (now about 4,000 feet above sea level) with lava and ash. 5) To remind people of the caldera's volcanic origin, garnish with a 2,600-foot-tall lava cone (Wizard Island). 6) Add water (nearly 4.6 trillion gallons) from rain and snowmelt until the lake reaches a depth of 1,932 feet. 7) Glaze with forty-five feet of snow each winter. Recipe serves 500,000 visitors (annually).

According to William G. Steel who led the move to create Oregon's only National Park nearly a century ago, "All ingenuity of nature seems to have been exerted to the fullest capacity to build a grand awe-inspiring temple the likes of which the world has never seen before." Established in 1902, the 286-square-mile park protects a gem, the world's seventh-deepest lake, and its high-country, volcanic setting. According to Klamath Indian legends, the bluebird was black prior to dipping its wings into the lake's waters. The Klamath considered the lake sacred and kept its existence secret from the white man until a party of gold-seekers happened upon it in 1853. They called it Deep Blue Lake, in recognition of its mid-oceanlike color. Because of the lake's youth and the fact that no streams drain into the lake (all the land outside the rim slopes away), Crater Lake's waters are the world's clearest, unimpaired even by hydrothermal venting from the lake bottom.

Mt. Mazama's cataclysmic eruption was forty-two times more powerful than that of Mt. St. Helens in 1980. In the 7,700 years since, trees have recolonized much of the surrounding area, but there is ample evidence of vulcanism in the form of lava fields and cinder cones. Altitude, heavy snowfall, and wind have stunted the whitebark pine along the crater rim where snow lingers into July, most years. Wildlife, including black bear, bobcat, deer, and marmots have also returned. The lake has two species of fish, the landlocked kokanee salmon and rainbow trout, both introduced by Mr. Steel.

About five hours drive from Portland and eight from San Francisco, Crater Lake has brief summers because of the high snowfall. Although the park is open year round, often the thirty-three mile Rim Drive is not completely open until mid-July and closes again in October; the North Entrance Road is also closed in winter. With the clean air that prevails at 7,000 feet, visibility from the crater rim often exceeds one hundred miles. The Pacific Crest Trail, which runs from Canada to Mexico, cuts across the Park from north to south; eight other trails range from easy strolls to strenuous climbs. Provided they can climb the 700 feet back to the rim, summer visitors should hike down to the lake and take a boat tour at Cleetwood Cove.

—Mike Macy

The rising sun reaches the rim of Crater Lake, viewed from Watchman Peak.

The white snow rimming Crater Lake makes its famously blue waters appear even more vivid.

Whitebark pine is stunted by high >>> altitude and heavy snowfall.

Olympic

FOLDOUT: **Remnants of the headlands, eroded by pounding surf, stand sentinel on Rialto Beach at sunset.**

THEORETICALLY, THE OLYMPIC MOUNTAINS WERE SO NAMED because they reminded Juan de Fuca—who was exploring the West Coast for Portugal in 1592—of the Olympic Mountains (said to be the home of the gods) in his ancestral Greece. Although de Fuca's claim of discovery is questioned, the label is apt; the Olympic Peninsula offers nearly everything a god could want: surf-pounded beaches, headlands, and arches; cathedral-like temperate rain forests; subalpine meadows awash with wildflowers; and glacier-clad summits.

While the adjacent waters had become a locus of exploration by the 1770s, the peninsula's interior remained largely unexplored until the 1880s. By 1890, however, the few people who had ventured into the heart of the Olympics were already calling for its protection. Army Lieutenant Joseph O'Neil, leader of the first documented expedition into the interior, noted in 1890 that "It would...serve admirably for a national park. There are numerous elk, that noble animal so fast disappearing from this country, that should be protected." These gentle, 500-pound herbivores were being slaughtered solely for their eye teeth, which were valued as watch fobs. The Olympic Forest Reserve, including most of peninsula's forests, was created by President Cleveland in 1897. President Theodore Roosevelt established Mount Olympus National Monument in 1909, protecting the peninsula's core and its elk (subsequently named in his honor). In 1938 President Franklin D. Roosevelt signed legislation creating Olympic National Park. Midway in size between Rhode Island and Delaware, the 1,440-square-mile park consists of a mountainous center, the Queets River Corridor, and a sixty-mile long coastal strip, which was added in 1953.

In 1858 the usually understated U.S. Coast Survey called the Olympic forest "an immeasurable sea of gigantic timber coming down to the very shores." Today, the park contains some of the largest and best remnants of the old-growth, temperate rain forests that formerly stretched along the Pacific Coast from Oregon to Alaska. Rising to 7,965 feet within thirty miles of the ocean, the Olympic Mountains protect the coast from cold continental air masses while intercepting moisture moving in from the Pacific. The southwest corner of the park receives as much as seventeen feet of precipitation annually, more than any other area in the Lower 48 states. The resultant rain forest, which one early visitor dubbed "a splendid confusion," consists of tangles of vine maple, brambles, and devil's club; profusions of mosses and ferns on the ground and high above in the red alder and big leaf maple; and the coniferous canopy of Sitka Spruce, western hemlock, Douglas fir, and western redcedar. The peninsula harbors record- and near-record-size trees of more than half a dozen species, and Sitka spruce can reach heights of 300 feet. Tree species on the peninsula's east side are completely different; the mountains remove moisture so thoroughly from passing weather systems that the town of Sequin, just northeast of the park, receives only seventeen inches of rain per year.

The Olympics consist largely of sandstones, shales, and lavas deposited on the Pacific Ocean bottom about 30 million years ago. As the plate carrying the Pacific Ocean bottom slid under the plate carrying the North American continent, these rocks were scraped off, folded, and domed up. The subsequent erosion of this dome by glaciers and rivers created the peninsula's pattern of rivers radiating outward from the central core. During the last Ice Age, great glaciers sweeping out of the Cascades isolated the peninsula from the mainland, with the curious result that it has sixteen species not found elsewhere and lacks eleven species found across Puget Sound in the Cascades. Missing species include grizzly bear, porcupine, and mountain sheep. Endemic species include the Olympic marmot, Olympic pocket gopher, and the Beardslee and Crescenti trout. The last of the peninsula's timber wolves were exterminated in the 1930s, but cougar and black bear help keep the populations of varied hare, Columbia blacktail deer, and Roosevelt elk in check. Introduced in the 1920s, mountain goat have resisted control by predators and are damaging alpine and subalpine flora.

The park is two hours by car and ferry from Seattle, and five from Portland, Oregon. Thirteen spike roads lead up the valleys, but none cross the park. Two roads climb into the subalpine zone. In seventeen miles, the Hurricane Ridge Road climbs from sea level to 5,000 feet, providing commanding views of Mount Olympus, the Elwha Valley, Port Angeles, and Vancouver Island. Visitors should plan on spending at least one day on the park's north side and one day on the west. In addition to numerous self-guided nature trails, 600 miles of trails make Olympic a hiker's paradise.

—Mike Macy

ShiShi Beach

Mount Olympus viewed from the High Divide, Blue Glacier

Vine maple and moss in the Hoh rain forest

Mount Rainier

CAPTAIN GEORGE VANCOUVER, WHILE MAPPING PUGET SOUND for Britain in 1792, is credited with being the first European to have seen Mount Rainier, which he described as "a remarkably high mountain covered with snow " and named for a friend, Rear Admiral Peter Rainier, who never saw it. The neighboring Indian tribes already had a name for it, "Tahoma" meaning "the mountain that was God." At 14,411 feet, Rainier so dominates the surrounding 6,000-foot peaks that even in Seattle when people talk about "the mountain," everybody knows which of the hundreds visible from the city they mean. For more than a century, Mount Rainier has been a magnet for climbers, both for the challenge and for what John Muir, in 1888 a member of the sixth party to summit it, called "its vast, map-like views." In 1886 George B. Bayley, one of Rainier's earliest climbers, wrote, "The view from the top was inexpressibly grand and comprehensive, although the whole landscape below an altitude of 5,000 feet was swallowed up in a sea of vapor, leaving the higher mountains standing out like islands." The park was created in 1899 to protect Rainier, the tallest volcano in the Cascade Range, which stretches from Mt. Garibaldi in Canada to Mt. Lassen in northern California.

About a million years old, the volcano was built by hundreds of eruptions. Geologists estimate that Rainier was as much as 2,000 feet higher before eruptions, landslides, and glaciers reduced it to its current size. Mt.

Rainier last erupted about a hundred years ago. Although there are steam vents in its summit crater, it is currently considered dormant, but that could change, as Mount St. Helens, its neighbor to the south, showed with its dramatic eruption in 1980.

Rainier makes its own weather by intercepting moisture moving in off the Pacific Ocean. Averaging over 600 inches of snow each year, the mountain set a North American snowfall record with 1,122 inches in the winter of 1971–72. This snow feeds twenty-five glaciers, the largest collection on a single mountain in the Lower 48 states. Snow lingers through mid-summer at 5,000 feet, watering meadows of wildflowers. Black bear, cougar, marmot, deer, Roosevelt elk (introduced in the early 1900s), and mountain goat make their homes in the park. Impressed by carpets of glacier and avalanche lily, shooting star, paintbrush, lupine and pungent bear grass, Elcaine Longmire, an early resident of the area said, "This must be what Paradise is like!" Her exclamation became the name of the subalpine lodge and visitor center from which most summit climbs begin. Below 3,000 feet, much of the moisture falls as rain, creating lush temperate rain forests on the western flanks. To the east, the mountain casts a pronounced rain shadow.

Because it is less than three hours from Seattle, traffic can be intense, particularly on weekends when it may seem as if all of the 1,800,00 annual visitors chose the same day to see the park. At 367 square miles, the park is one-third the size of Rhode Island. With the exception of the northwest corner, roads make it possible to drive most of the way around the mountain in summer. Park nature trails at Longmire, Carbon River, and Ohanapecosh offer opportunities to experience Rainier's rain forests. Paradise features wildflowers, and Sunrise, the highest point reachable by car, is the best place to obtain a sense of how big the mountain is. A ninety-three mile hiking trail circles the mountain. The broken tree trunks visible from the road in the Kautz Creek Valley resulted from a glacial outburst, which roared down the mountain in 1947.

—Mike Macy

LEFT: **Forest near Comet Falls**

RIGHT: **Lupines in Paradise Meadow**

View of Mt. Ranier from Sunrise Park

Yellow monkey flowers at Sunbeam Creek

Haleakala

IF HAWAII VOLCANOES NATIONAL PARK ON THE ISLAND OF Hawaii is the best place in the U.S. to see active volcanoes, Haleakala National Park on Maui, the next island north, is the best place to see what happens after the fireworks. Haleakala, which last erupted in 1790, is now dormant, but it could erupt in the future. The 10,023-foot peak dominates the island of Maui, sheltering in the climb to its summit "house of the sun," layers of such ecological diversity, that it was designated an International Biosphere Reserve in 1980.

Haleakala emerged from the sea more than 900,000 years ago. Over the next 500,000 years, eruptions gradually built up the volcano until it was several thousand feet higher than it is today. During the last 400,000 years, the erosive power of rainfall, wind, and possibly glaciation has outpaced vulcanism. Haleakala's biological diversity derives from the interaction of two factors: variations in altitude and rainfall. First, the mountain rises abruptly from subtropical sea level through several life zones to its alpine summit. Second, the prevailing trade winds drench the east side of the volcano with up to 400 inches of rain a year, while the western slopes receive between twenty and forty inches of rain per year.

Moving westward over the top of the mountain from Kipahulu at the southeast corner of the park, one encounters in order a lowland coastal forest, a rain forest, a subalpine shrubland, the aeolian/alpine zone on top, more subalpine shrubland, and finally, dry forest. Only a few isolated pockets of lowland coastal forest have survived 1,500 years of human activities and introduced species. However, more of the rain forest remains, with ohi'a and koa trees forming a canopy and smaller trees, ferns, shrubs, and herbs forming the understory. The rain forest is home to numerous rare and endangered birds, insects, and spiders. The subalpine shrubland supports more than a dozen species of shrubs and grasses and provides a home for many bird species, including the endangered *nene*, or Hawaiian goose. Although the alpine/aeolian (windy) zone receives plenty of rainfall, the moisture sinks rapidly into the mostly bare ground or evaporates quickly when the sun is shining. From a car, the alpine/aeolian zone appears barren and desertlike, but closer examination reveals that the ground is alive with spiders and insects and a few species of plants, including the cactuslike *ahinahina*, or silversword. Reduced in extent by cattle, goats, and wildfire, the park's only surviving dry forest is in the Kaupo Gap.

Haleakala shelters exceedingly rare species that have evolved to Hawaiian conditions over hundreds of thousands of years. Many Hawaiian species have been less successful in adapting to the rapid changes caused by exotic species brought by Polynesian seafarers in the past 1,500 years. At least eighty-five species of birds have been extinguished, but two honeycreepers, the 'I'iwi and the Apapane, have been able to adapt. These gorgeous crimson honeycreepers are often seen on Haleakala, as are endangered *nene*, the *ppeo*, or Hawaiian short-eared owl, and the *'ua'u*, or dark-rumped petrel.

Most park visitors drive the switchback road from Kahului to watch the sun rise and gaze into the summit crater. Haleakala's crater was not created by vulcanism, but by erosion, and so is not considered a true crater. Trails lead through the crater, but rapidly changing weather, rapid elevation changes, and high altitude make hiking here extremely challenging.

The isolation of the southeastern corner of the park has helped preserve aspects of traditional Hawaiian life. Ohe'o Gulch, the waterfall-fed stream that spills down the terraces of a lava flow to the pounding surf below is a fine place to spot humpback whales.

—Mike Macy

Rain-fed waterfalls of Pipiwai Stream have carved multiple terraces into ancient lava in Ohe'o Gulch.

Haleakala Crater

When fog does not obscure the sight of the sun rising over Haleakala, it is obvious why thousands of tourists drive to its summit in the pre-dawn darkness to witness the spectacle.

Hawaii Volcanoes

THERE ARE FEW PLACES IN THE WORLD WHERE THE REAL estate truism—that they aren't making more of it—doesn't hold. One is the island of Hawaii, called the Big Island because it is already the largest of the chain. Mother Nature regularly enlarges the Big Island using volcanic materials from deep beneath the Pacific Ocean floor. Southernmost island in the 1,500-mile-long Emperor Seamount-Hawaiian Island Chain, Hawaii is also the tallest and youngest. For the past 70 to 80 million years, the Pacific Plate has been moving northwestward about four inches per year over a hot spot in the earth's mantle. As long as the Big Island occupies this hot seat, Mother Nature, or *Pele*, the Hawaiian fire goddess, will continue to deliver molten lava to the surface where it can flow

downhill, creating new real estate when it reaches the Pacific Ocean. Meanwhile, Lo'ihi, an undersea volcano thirty-two miles south of Hawaii's southern tip, gradually grows toward the surface and will someday replace the Big Island as the chain's youngest and southernmost landmass.

Hawaii Volcanoes National Park was created in 1916 to protect Mauna Loa and Kilauea volcanoes on the Big Island and Haleakala on Maui. (To improve management, Haleakala became a separate national park in 1961.) Today, Hawaii Volcanoes is also an International Biosphere Reserve and World Heritage Site. Considered the world's most massive mountain, Mauna Loa has a volume of at least 18,000 cubic miles and may also be the

world's tallest: Mauna Loa rises almost 32,000 feet from the sea floor to its summit, 13,677 feet above sea level. Mauna Loa has erupted at least five times since 1942, most recently in 1984. Located on Mauna Loa's east flank, 4,096-foot Kilauea has been erupting almost continually since 1970. As Hawaiian lavas are more viscous, or liquid, than lavas associated with diving plate boundaries, eruptions here are generally less explosive. As a result of the frequency and tranquility of their eruptions, Mauna Loa and Kilauea are the world's most studied and best understood volcanoes. In the late 1980s at Kilauea, scientists were able for the first time to observe and film underwater lava pouring into the sea, confirming the long-held theory that pillow basalts are formed under water.

While only a few hours drive from most Big Island resorts, Hawaii Volcanoes experiences all kinds of weather, from tropical heat to frigid rains at Kilauea and snow high on Mauna Loa. Because successive Kilauea lava floes over the last century can be accurately dated, visitors can gain a sense of the plant and animal recolonization that begins almost as soon as the lava surface cools with the arrival of insects and the growth of lichens and ferns. The rapid return of dense forest demonstrates the old saw that "nature abhors a vacuum."

Over millions of years, plants, animals, and insects from all corners of the Pacific arrived by wind, ocean current, and wing to colonize and evolve in the Hawaiian Island chain. As a result, 90 percent of fauna and flora

currently native to Hawaii is endemic, or found nowhere else. After evolving from a few common ancestors, many of these species are now threatened by more recent arrivals like pigs, cats, goats, rats, and mongoose that were introduced by man in the past 1,500 years. Some of the endemic species commonly seen by park visitors include the *nene*, or Hawaiian goose, and the *Io*, or Hawaiian hawk. Because the nearest continental land mass (North America) is more than 2,500 miles away, very few native Hawaiian species are found elsewhere. An exception is the *kolea*, or golden plover. Breeding on the Alaskan tundra and wintering in grassy areas throughout the Hawaiian chain, the golden plover flies the 2,800 miles to and from Alaska non-stop in three to four days.

—Mike Macy

Steam pours from a vent on Kilauea, which is one of >>> the most active volcanoes in the world.

A river of fire flows down the flanks of Kilauea.

A new lava flow steams as it hits the ocean near Wahaula.